AUGSBURG HISTORICAL ATLAS

AUGSBURG HISTORICAL ATLAS

of christianity in the middle ages and reformation

by Charles S. Anderson

AUGSBURG PUBLISHING HOUSE

Minneapolis, Minnesota

Dedicated with gratitude
and affection to my students,
Luther Theological Seminary,
St. Paul, Minnesota

AUGSBURG HISTORICAL ATLAS
OF CHRISTIANITY IN THE MIDDLE AGES AND REFORMATION

Copyright © 1967 Augsburg Publishing House

Library of Congress Catalog Card No. 67-11723

Manufactured in the United States of America

INTRODUCTION

*History without geography wanders as
a vagrant without certain habitation*

For several years I have been aware of the need of a working atlas for the study of Medieval and Reformation Church History. Most studies that deal with the period emphasize political and economic history at the expense of the religious, and maps that are pertinent are scattered and of widely varying value. Having convinced myself, and a publisher, that crude mimeographed drawings are not adequate cartographic tools, I began this project five years ago, reading as widely as possible on the subjects to be covered and collecting maps and drawings from every available source. The end result of this effort is before you.

The word "atlas" has come to mean a collection of maps, plates, and copious commentary. One thinks of the *Westminster Bible Atlas,* or Grollenberg's *Atlas of the Bible,* or the magnificent work on the ancient church by F. van der Meer and Christine Mohrmann, *The Atlas of the Early Christian World.* The volume which you hold in your hands is a much more modest effort. It aims simply to provide the student with relatively inexpensive working maps for use in conjunction with standard history texts, as e.g. Williston Walker's *History of the Christian Church.* Every attempt has been made to keep the cost at a reasonable level. For example, geographic details are not repeated on each succeeding plate; it is assumed that one can always refer back to the first one in the series. Only those elements which are thought essential are on each plate, i.e. not every town or even every major city may appear. This practice has the additional advantage of focusing the attention of the reader on essentials. Its disadvantage is that the author may err in his judgment of what is most important. I am open to attack and correction on this matter of judgment.

When speaking of possible omissions one must certainly acknowledge that this volume is at least as myopic as its predecessors in its almost exclusive concentration on the western church. The story of certain eastern groups has been ignored as if the only movements of significance occurred between the Mediterranean and the Arctic Circle. Hopefully another edition may one day correct this and picture for example the Monophysites of Egypt, Nubia, Ethiopia, and Syria who were contemporaries of both Gregory I and Charles the Great.

Perhaps we might then also look at the vast expanse of land covered by Nestorian missionaries, extending from the Caspian Sea to India, Ceylon, and even China by the seventh century. The great story of the Russian Church is certainly not adequately portrayed by simply noting the lines of mission expansion to the area, as we have done. Here also a selection has been made, hopefully to be amended and supplemented later.

No one begins *de novo* in an effort such as this. The visitor to my office will find standard map works scattered all over. Volumes by men like Muir, Shepherd, Putzger, and Heussi and Mulert have been studied and used. The greater part of the basic information, however, has come from the texts, both primary and secondary, that describe the various phenomena that make up the Middle Ages and the Reformation. I also gratefully acknowledge the helpful comments at the early stages of this project from colleagues and friends like Drs. W. Pauck, T. Tappert, P. Nyholm, B. Holm, E. Fevold, E. C. Nelson, and Hal Koch. Whatever credit accrues is to be shared with them and others; if there are errors and offense the blame is mine. Thanks also to John Mosand, the project artist, who took my rather crude drawing and scribbled notes and made of them the tool you have before you. Certainly the publisher should also be thanked for supporting a work that is not guaranteed to turn a handsome profit.

So here you have it: a labor of no small love, a volume modest in scope and execution, yet colorful enough for interest and accurate enough for value. Its texts are long enough for thinking and review; its margins wide enough for scribbling and rebuke.

It's your book now—a tool along with others. Please *do* think and review, scribble and rebuke.

Charles L Anderson

April, 1967

5

CONTENTS

Astrolabe, old navigational instrument— 10th to 17th Centuries

CONTENTS

THE TOPOGRAPHY OF EUROPE

Detail of a 1645 map of the Baltic Sea

Often in the study of history the facts of simple, physical geography are overlooked; but only at one's peril. Everything that follows in this volume is related to, and in a sense dictated by, the material of this first plate. One should, therefore, study it with some care.

Look at the river systems. In addition to draining the continent they provided lines for the commerce which in turn produced the great cities. The commercial cities on such trade avenues were the scenes of the appearance of a middle class that helped break down the static orders of medieval society. The rivers also served as routes of invasion. When the Viking ships swept out of the foggy north in the tenth century they turned their dragon-headed prows up the rivers in search of plunder. Off on another frontier, when Suleiman the Magnificent turned toward Europe in the sixteenth century, he moved up the Danube, and his heavy equipment came by boat. The rivers also provided protection for frontiers. The legions of Rome had long since used the Danube and the Rhine as bastions in their defense walls, and the Franks were later protected by the Elbe from the incursions of the Avars.

The mountain systems are of incalculable significance for our period. They so limited the arable lands in the north that the men were literally forced to take to the sea, to explore, plunder, and colonize. The peoples along the shore of the Mediterranean were protected by their mountains in many instances and also turned toward the sea. The Pyrenees and the Alps partially wall off the Iberian and Italian peninsulas. Other peoples were protected by the walls of nature: the Byzantine Empire sheltered behind the Taurus Range after being defeated in the eighth century; Hungary has a natural eastern border in the Carpathians; minor ranges tend to isolate and protect Bohemia.

Passes through the mountains became crucial possessions. These were the routes of movement, commercial or military. A small but determined force could hold up a whole army in a mountain pass. Along the routes of overland trade, as along the rivers, cities sprang up, providing a new and potent force in the Middle Ages.

One notes the plains, the arable lands that became so often a prize of competing monarchs (e.g. Francis I and Charles V). The plains also were often open avenues of march. The great north European plain provided a wide road to many invaders, including the Huns.

PLATE 1

EUROPE IN THE TIME OF GREGORY THE GREAT (590-604)

When Gregory reluctantly assumed the papal throne in 590 he inherited a church that was strong and wealthy, but also a society that had disintegrated. The walls of the great Roman Empire had long since been breached by successive waves of barbarian invasion and immigration. By Gregory's day the Lombards had established themselves in both the north and south of Italy, with their capital in Pavia. Only the corridor between Rome and Ravenna remained open as part of the Empire. Lombard pressure was a daily fact of life for Pope Gregory. His life, as he put it, was passed "among the swords of the Lombards."

In the north the descendants of Clovis (baptized 496) had extended the borders of the Frankish Empire. Farther north the warlike Saxons and Frisians held off all attempts of conquest. To the east the Avars, descendants of Mongols and the White Huns, were restive and by 562 had moved as far as the Elbe River where they met the Franks.

The Roman Empire had little or no power in the west. The representative of the Emperor hid behind the marshes at Ravenna and protested when the Pope presumed to do battle and even negotiate with his Lombard foes. Gregory appointed military governors to stem the tide, negotiated a peace with the Duke of Spoleto, and when King Agilulf marched toward Rome from Pavia, led the defense of the city. In 595 Gregory negotiated a peace with Agilulf, which outraged the emperor but which also made the Pope of greater significance in western politics than either the emperor or his exarch.

Since the Council of Chalcedon (451) five great centers or patriarchates had been recognized as providing leadership for Christendom. Rome was recognized as "first among equals," but there was a constant rivalry for preeminence between the Italian city and Constantinople that already foreshadowed the schism that would be finalized in 1054. Rome continued to grow in stature for a number of reasons: e.g. she was free from imperial domination during much of her history; she had a reputation for steadfastness in trouble, generosity, and orthodoxy that ran back for centuries; and she was reputed to have had two apostles labor and die within her walls, Peter and Paul. She was also blessed with strong leaders at crucial times. Gregory the Great was one of them.

PLATE 2

THE TOPOGRAPHY OF EUROPE

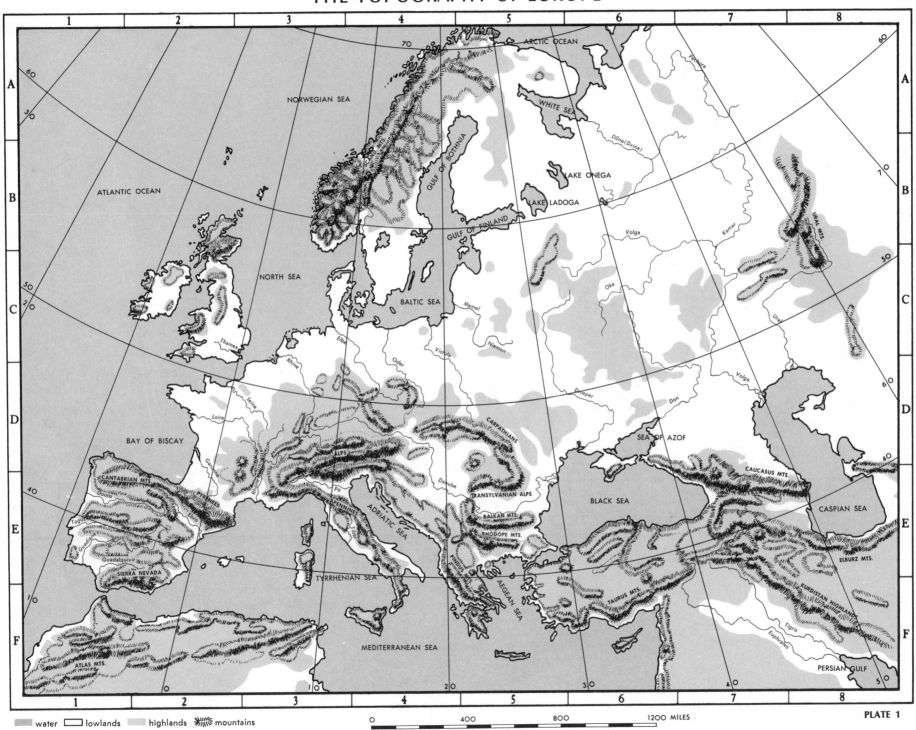

ATLANTIC OCEAN

NORWEGIAN SEA

ARCTIC OCEAN

WHITE SEA

Pechora

Düna (Dvina)

LAKE ONEGA

LAKE LADOGA

GULF OF BOTHNIA

GULF OF FINLAND

Volga

Kama

URAL MTS.

NORTH SEA

BALTIC SEA

Memel

Niemen

Oka

Ural

Thames

Elbe

Vistula

Oder

Dnieper

Don

Volga

Rhine

Seine

Loire

BAY OF BISCAY

CARPATHIANS

SEA OF AZOF

CANTABRIAN MTS.

Douro

Garonne

Rhône

ALPS

Danube

TRANSYLVANIAN ALPS

CAUCASUS MTS.

BLACK SEA

PYRENEES

Po

APENNINES

Tiber

ADRIATIC SEA

BALKAN MTS.

CASPIAN SEA

Tagus

Ebro

RHODOPE MTS.

ELBURZ MTS.

Guadiana

Guadalquivir

SIERRA NEVADA

TYRRHENIAN SEA

PINDUS

AEGEAN SEA

TAURUS MTS.

KURDISTAN HIGHLAND

Tigris

Euphrates

ATLAS MTS.

MEDITERRANEAN SEA

PERSIAN GULF

9

water ▨ lowlands ☐ highlands ▨ mountains ☀

PLATE 1

0   400   800   1200 MILES

EUROPE IN THE TIME OF GREGORY THE GREAT (590-604)

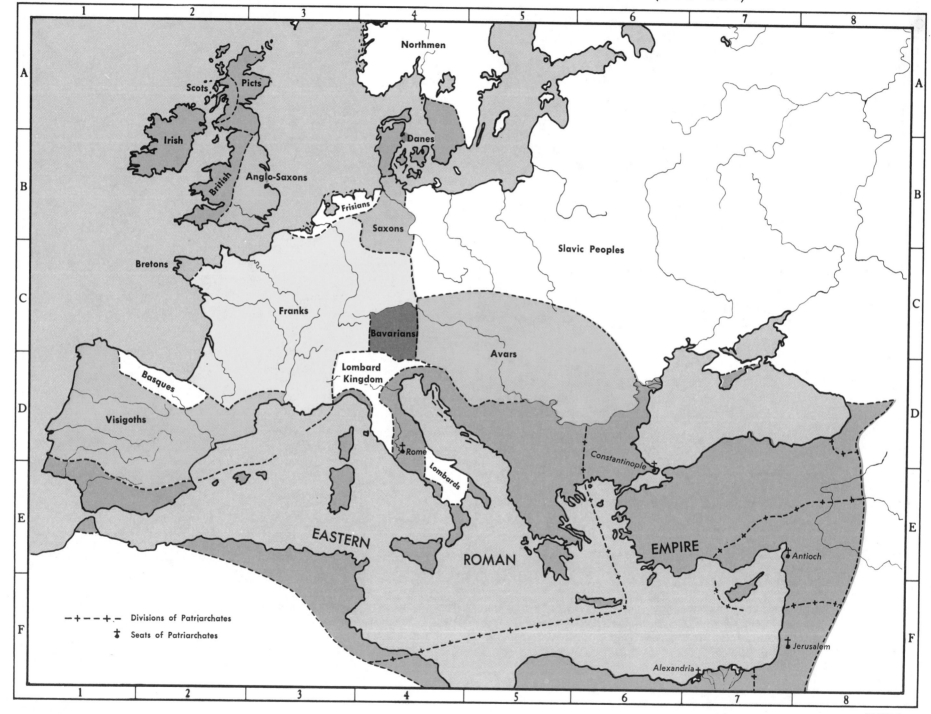

Northmen

Scots
Picts

Irish

British
Anglo-Saxons

Frisians

Danes

Saxons

Slavic Peoples

Bretons

Franks

Bavarians

Avars

Basques

Lombard
Kingdom

Visigoths

Rome

Constantinople

Lombards

EASTERN

ROMAN

EMPIRE

Antioch

Jerusalem

Alexandria

– + – + – Divisions of Patriarchates

✝ Seats of Patriarchates

PLATE 2

CHRISTIANITY AMONG BRITISH AND GERMANIC PEOPLES

There were Christians in Britain by the third century, but after the withdrawal of Roman troops in 410 there was a relapse into near paganism as the British form of the faith was driven back toward Wales and Ireland by the onrushing waves of barbarian invaders. The islands had to be missionized again.

Both Celtic (i.e. British) and Roman forces participated in the island effort. The great name in Irish Christian history is Patrick. A third generation Christian whose whole life is overlaid with legend, Patrick came to Ireland as a missionary around 432. The Christianity he fostered was tribal rather than diocesan in organization and laid strong emphasis on monastic communities which were centers of learning and mission work. Though most of them would be destroyed by later invaders, the monastic houses were islands of culture for years when Europe was squatting in the shadows of ignorance. Impelled by zeal for the faith and wanderlust, many mission expeditions set out from the Celtic centers. In the sixth century (565) Columba crossed over from Ireland to Scotland and established a beachhead for mission work on the island of Iona. The next century Aidan (634) followed the same pattern as he founded Lindesfarne on the eastern coast. From these two centers the Celtic form gradually spread to much of England. Not content to work so close to home, some Celtic missionaries traveled to the continent. The best example of such work is in the figure of Columbanus.

In 596 the Roman monk Augustine, having been sent by Pope Gregory I, arrived in southern England with several companions. His concern was not only for the conversion of the English, but for their acceptance of the Roman form of the faith rather than the Celtic. Paganism did succumb, but the struggle with the indigenous form of Christianity was not resolved until 664 when Rome triumphed at the Synod of Whitby.

While some Frankish work had been done along the Rhine, the real mission thrust to the Germans came from the British. Great names such as Wilfrid and Willibrord should be remembered, along with the greatest, Winfrid, or Boniface (d. 754, 5). Boniface founded Christianity among the Germans east of the Rhine, organized the church there, and introduced the Benedictine Rule. He also helped reform the Frankish church and brought nearly all of western Europe under papal control.

PLATE 3

MISSIONS TO SCANDINAVIA AND EASTERN EUROPE

The name of Anskar (d. 865) is inextricably associated with Christianity in Denmark and Sweden. Going first as a missionary monk to Denmark in 827 and to Sweden in 830, he later became Archbishop of Hamburg, with missionary responsibility for the North. Second mission trips to Denmark (851) and Sweden (852) saw the decline of paganism and the rise of a well-established Christian community. After Anskar's death, however, there was a pagan reaction and it was not until the second half of the tenth century that real progress again was made. King Harald Bluetooth was baptized in 950 and under his grandson, Cnute, Denmark became officially Christian.

Christianity in Norway was first effectively introduced by Olaf Tryggvesson (d. 1000) and Olaf Haraldsson (d. 1030). The first church was established at Møster, and a period of forced conversion followed (995-999). The choice was "battle or baptism" under Tryggvesson. Haraldsson invaded Norway in 1016, intent on the complete Christianization of the country. He was killed at the battle of Stiklestad in 1030. The forces of Christianity were, however, firmly rooted by this time, due to royal initiative on the one hand and the work of missionaries from England on the other. Sweden's paganism was the last in the three major Scandinavian lands to succumb, and this only in the twelfth century.

In the east and south towns like Passau and Salzburg served as mission centers on the pagan frontier, as did Sirmium from which Cyril and Methodius moved out into Moravia. Both German expansionist tendencies and missionary zeal contributed to the work of the church in areas like Poland and among peoples like the Magyars.

The Baltic areas only gradually came under Christian influence through the efforts of men like the elderly German monk Meinhard and Otto of Bamberg. The conversion of this area was through German influence, sometimes by force, and was not really completed until the fifteenth century.

The church in Russia was first of all under Byzantine rather than Roman control. Christian influence grew after the conversion of Prince Vladimir (987) and centered at the capital, Kiev. The center of religious affairs moved to Moscow after Kiev fell to the Mongols in 1237. Some of the great monastic centers in Russia were also effective mission outposts.

PLATE 4

Celtic Cross, c. 9th Century

Elaborately carved crosses like this are among the few remaining monuments of a once vigorous Christian community

CHRISTIANITY AMONG BRITISH AND GERMANIC PEOPLES

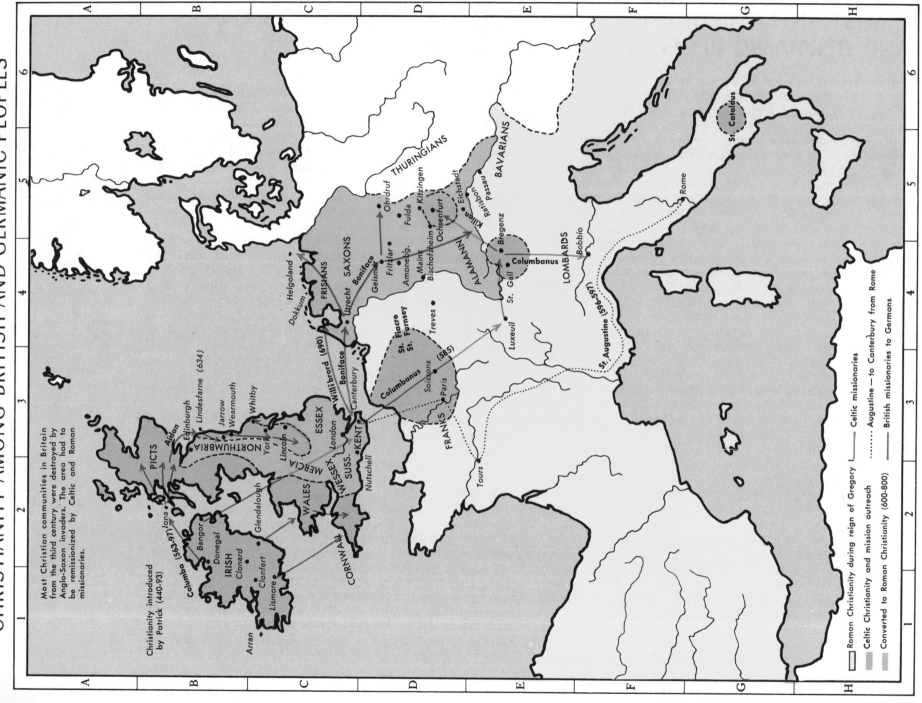

Most Christian communities in Britain from the third century were destroyed by Anglo-Saxon invaders. The area had to be remissionized by Celtic and Roman missionaries.

Christianity introduced by Patrick (440-93)

PICTS

Columba (563-97) Iona

Arran

IRISH

Bangor

Donegal

Clonard

Clonfert

Lismore

Glendalough

WALES

CORNWALL

Aidan

Edinburgh

Lindesfarne (634)

Jarrow

Wearmouth

Whitby

NORTHUMBRIA

York

Lincoln

MERCIA

ESSEX

London

WESSEX

SUSS.

KENT

Canterbury

Nutschell

Boniface

Willibrord (690)

Utrecht

Dokkum

Helgoland

FRISIANS

SAXONS

Boniface

Geismar

Ohrdruf

THURINGIANS

Fritzlar

Fulda

Amoneb.

Mainz

Bischofsheim

Kitzingen

Ochsenfurt

Eichstadt

Kilian

Passau

Ratisbon

BAVARIANS

ALAMANNI

Biregenz

St. Gall

Columbanus

LOMBARDS

Bobbio

St. Fiacre

St. Furnsey

Treves

Soissons

Paris

Columbanus (585)

FRANKS

Luxeuil

Tours

St. Augustine (596-597)

Rome

St. Cataldus

Legend

Roman Christianity during reign of Gregory

Celtic Christianity and mission outreach

Converted to Roman Christianity (600-800)

Celtic missionaries

Augustine — to Canterbury from Rome

British missionaries to Germans

PLATE 3

MISSIONS TO SCANDINAVIA AND EASTERN EUROPE

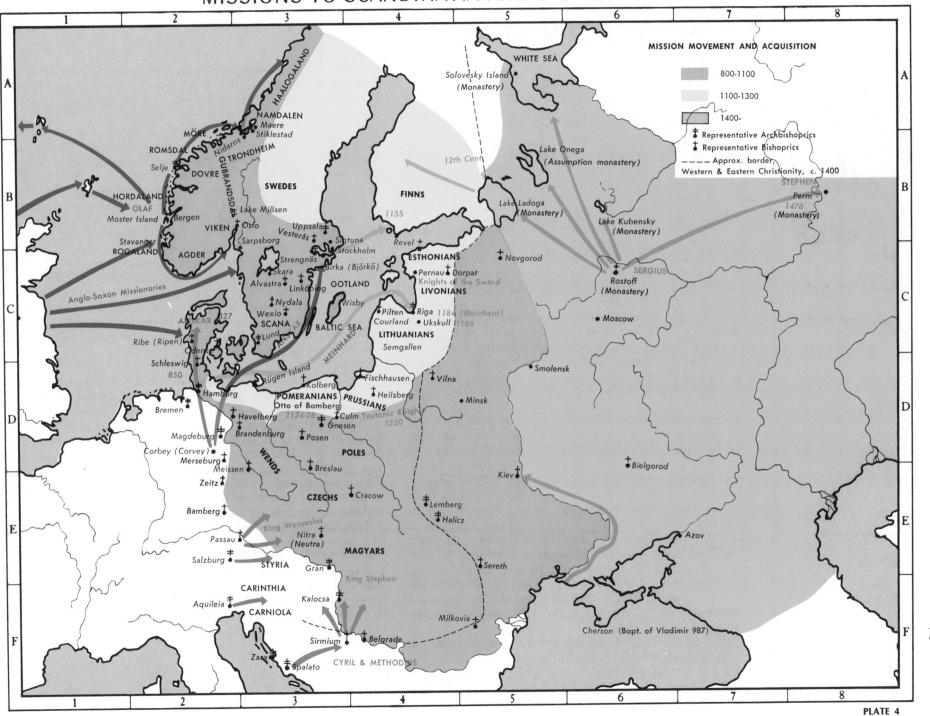

MISSION MOVEMENT AND ACQUISITION

800-1100

1100-1300

1400-

‡ Representative Archbishoprics
† Representative Bishoprics
--- Approx. border, Western & Eastern Christianity, c. 1400

WHITE SEA

Soloviesky Island (Monastery)

12th Cent.

Lake Onega (Assumption monastery)

STEPHEN

Perm 1478 (Monastery)

Lake Ladoga (Monastery)

Lake Kubensky (Monastery)

HAALOGALAND

NAMDALEN
Maere
Stiklestad
MÖRE
ROMSDAL
Nidaros
TRONDHEIM
Selje
DOVRE
GUBRANDSDAL

SWEDES

FINNS
1155

HORDALAND
OLAF
Moster Island
Bergen
VIKEN
Oslo
Sarpsborg
Lake Mjösen
Uppsala
Vesterås
Sigtuna
Stockholm
Revel

Novgorod

SERGIUS

Rostoff (Monastery)

STAVANGER
ROGALAND
AGDER

Strengnäs
Skara
Alvastra
Birka (Björkö)
Linköping
GOTLAND
ESTHONIANS
Pernau
Dorpat
Knights of the Sword
LIVONIANS

Moscow

Anglo-Saxon Missionaries

ANSKAR 827
Nydala
Wexio
SCANA
Lund
Wisby
BALTIC SEA
Pilten
Courland
Riga 1184 (Meinhard)
Ukskull 1186
LITHUANIANS
Semgallen

Rib (Ripen)
Odense
Schleswig 850
Hamburg
Rügen Island
Kolberg
POMERANIANS
Otto of Bamberg
1124-28
MEINHARD
Fischhausen
Heilsberg
PRUSSIANS
Culm
Teutonic Knights
1230
Vilna

Smolensk

Minsk

Bremen
Havelberg
Magdeburg
Brandenburg
Corbey (Corvey)
Merseburg
Meissen
Zeitz
WENDS
Gnesen
Posen
POLES
Breslau
Bielgorod

Kiev

Bamberg
CZECHS
Cracow
Lemberg
Halicz

King Wenceslas
Passau
Nitra (Neutra)
Salzburg
STYRIA
MAGYARS
Gran
King Stephen
Sereth

Azov

CARINTHIA
Aquileia
CARNIOLA
Kalocsa
Sirmium
Belgrade
Milkovia
Zara
Spalato
CYRIL & METHODIUS
Cherson (Bapt. of Vladimir 987)

13

PLATE 4

MOSLEM EXPANSION TO 1481

The Dome of the Rock, Jerusalem

The oldest Islamic building in existence

In the eighth century one of its gravest crises faced Christianity. After centuries of expansion she met an enemy that was dedicated, implacable, and utterly devoted to conquest for the sake of religion and race. Spawned in the great desert wastes of Arabia, molded and formed by Mohammed (d. 632), the forces of Islam swept over the Near East, North Africa, and into Europe itself by the eighth century. It was only at the battle of Poitiers (732) that the mounted horde was turned back from the heartland by Charles Martel and his Frankish cavalry. Driven back into the Iberian peninsula, they were entrenched there until 1492.

How could a disunited, largely nomadic collection of factious tribes become such a juggernaut of conquest? At least part of the answer lies in the genius of Mohammed who gathered together elements from the old paganism, from Christianity and Judaism, and created a system that claimed to complete and purify its constituent parts rather than rejecting them.

A fortunate set of historical circumstances also aided the movement. For example, the two great powers in the East, Byzantium and Persia, had fought each other to a standstill and were in no position to put down their upstart neighbor making warlike sounds in the South. Arab armies had also learned a great deal about warfare by serving the two colossi to the North.

By Mohammed's death (632) the Arabian Peninsula was united under the flag of Islam. His successor (or caliph), Abu Bakr, led the largely Bedouin armies against the Byzantine and Sasanian empires. The next caliph, Umar, extended the boundaries still further before his murder. The third caliph, Uthman, belonged to the Umayyad house, an aristocratic family from Mecca. This family was to become the most prominent in Islamic history. The Umayyad (Ommiad) caliphs, fourteen in number, ruled from Damascus until 750 and were succeeded by the Abbassids. At the murder of Uthman in 656, Ali, the only male descendant of Mohammed, became caliph. A split developed between those who favored a hereditary succession (the Shiites) and those who adhered to the tradition, the Sunna (the Sunnites). This division is perpetuated to this day in two competing theological systems.

Despite internal dissension the empire, partly religious, partly political and military, expanded until by the time of the Crusades it was a vast domain stretching from the Pyrenees to the Indus River. It was not, in its later years, ruled by one caliph. In the east the Seljuk Turks had overthrown the caliphs of Baghdad; in the center a schismatic religious group, the Caliphate of Cairo, held sway; while in the west the Almoravids, a Moorish people, governed.

As the years passed another force of significance appeared among the soldiers of Islam. In the thirteenth century the Seljuk ruler of Iconium was assisted in battle against a Mongol army by one Ertoghrul. The Seljuk rewarded him with a grant of land near the cities of Nicaea and Nicomedia. Ertoghrul died in 1288 and was succeeded by his son Osman. His descendants are known as the Ottoman Turks. Whether this people were Moslems before they left central Asia is a debated point. There is no doubt, however, that the Islamic faith played a major part in their later expansion. The plate indicates how the fingers of conquest were beginning to reach up into Europe. Since the first battle of Kossovo in 1389 Slavic resistance in the Balkans was nonexistent. Only Hungary and Venice stood between the Turks and Europe, and they were already beginning to decline by the late fifteenth and early sixteenth centuries. What happened when they no longer blocked the path can be seen by referring to plates 19 and 31.

The presence and power of these forces of Islam were irritating and alarming facts of life for Medieval and Reformation Europe. Turned back in the West, the pressure mounted in the East, and gradually the Byzantine lands were conquered, until finally, in 1453, Constantinople, the last great bastion of Eastern Christianity, fell. In succeeding years the pressure extended up into the Balkans and in Luther's day even the great city of Vienna was besieged (1529).

Christian Europe found herself involved in another way. In addition to attempting to defend her own borders, the great calls to free the Holy Land from the infidels stirred the continent for nearly two hundred years. (See plate 13.)

The Mediterranean became, in some periods, an Islamic lake. Speedy Moslem galleys scoured the sea and even landed in Italy and what is now the Riviera to establish permanent raiding bases. (See plate 7.) Not even the Alpine passes were safe from the raiders based at Garde Frainet. As we will note later, this type of incursion hastened the death of the once-great Carolingian empire.

PLATE 5

MOSLEM EXPANSION TO 1481

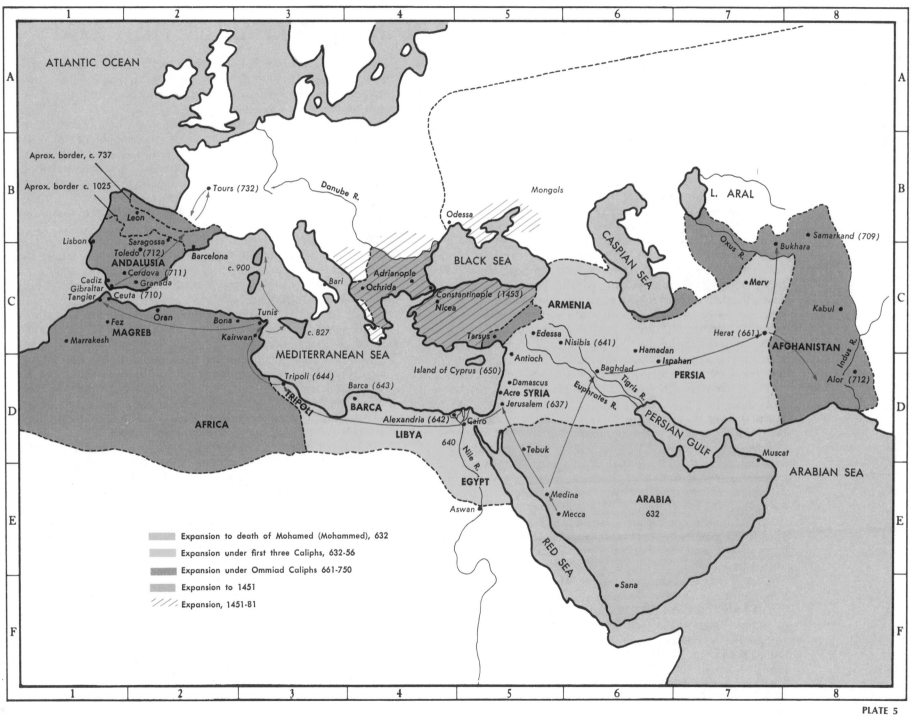

Aprox. border, c. 737

Aprox. border c. 1025

ATLANTIC OCEAN

Tours (732)
Danube R.
Mongols
L. ARAL
Leon
Lisbon
Saragossa
Toledo (712)
Barcelona
ANDALUSIA
c. 900
Cordova (711)
Cadiz
Granada
Gibraltar
Tangier   Ceuta (710)
Fez
Oran   Bona
MAGREB   Kairwan
Marrakesh
Tunis
c. 827
Bari
MEDITERRANEAN SEA
BLACK SEA
Adrianople
Ochrida
Constantinople (1453)
Nicea
ARMENIA
CASPIAN SEA
Samarkand (709)
Bukhara
Merv
Kabul
Herat (661)
AFGHANISTAN
Indus R.
Tarsus
Island of Cyprus (650)
Edessa
Nisibis (641)
Antioch
Hamadan
Ispahan
Baghdad
PERSIA
Alor (712)
Tripoli (644)
TRIPOLI
Barca (643)
BARCA
Damascus
Acre SYRIA
Jerusalem (637)
Euphrates R.
Tigris R.
PERSIAN GULF
Alexandria (642)   Cairo
AFRICA
LIBYA
640
Nile R.
Muscat
EGYPT
Tebuk
ARABIAN SEA
Aswan
Medina
ARABIA
632
RED SEA
Mecca
Sana

Expansion to death of Mohamed (Mohammed), 632

Expansion under first three Caliphs, 632-56

Expansion under Ommiad Caliphs 661-750

Expansion to 1451

Expansion, 1451-81

Odessa

15

PLATE 5

THE CAROLINGIAN EMPIRE IN THE TIME OF CHARLES THE GREAT

Investiture

Charles the Great invests Roland with the Spanish March
12th century drawing, Heidelberg University Library

In 771, at the death of his brother Carloman with whom he had shared the rule of their father's lands, Charles, son of Pepin the Short, became sole ruler of the Franks. He inherited a crown recently taken from the last of the Merovingian rulers through military strength and political maneuvering. Pepin and his forbears had ruled in fact for some time as Mayors of the Palace while the Merovingians, rulers in name, did nothing. Now, through negotiations with the Pope, it was agreed that the Franks would assist the papal throne against its enemies the Lombards, and in turn the Pope would legitimize Pepin's becoming in name what he already was in fact, i.e. ruler.

Perhaps a word about the background of this event would be in order. Charles Martel had refused to come to the aid of Pope Gregory III when the latter was under pressure from the Lombards. Rome had been sorely pressed again in the 750's, this time by the Lombard king, Aistulf. The Franks had a new ruler, the Mayor of the Palace, Pepin, who appealed for papal sanction to his act of deposing the last of the Merovingian rulers, Childeric III. Pope Zacharius concurred. Pepin was crowned and later fulfilled his part of the bargain as he moved south twice and not only defeated Aistulf but gave the conquered Lombard lands to the papacy. Thus began the "states of the church" which were to make the popes secular as well as ecclesiastical princes and involve them in all the maneuvering of power politics. One cannot understand the papacy of the Middle Ages without remembering the requirements of defense and acquisition that accompanied large land holdings in a feudal society. The papal lands were not lost until 1870.

Another result of the Pepin-papal arrangement was that a precedent now seemed to have been established that the popes had power to create secular rulers and were therefore above them. When there were strong secular rulers they continued to control the papacy, as Pepin did in fact, but the notion that the Pope made, or at least had to approve, the secular estate continued to live on in the minds of Catholic Europe. The fact that Charles the Great was crowned by the Pope supported this precedent.

Charles's accession (771) found the former parts of the Merovingian Kingdom united, i.e. Neustria, Austrasia, Burgundy, and Aquitaine. He began a series of military actions that earned the accolade "the Great" which has been attached to his name. From 771 to c. 800 he led over fifty campaigns. The Saxons, Slavs, Lombards, Bavarians, and Moslems all felt his sword. He reached out until over half of Italy, almost half of modern Germany and Austria-Hungary, all of modern France, Belgium, and Holland, and a part of northern Spain were parts of his empire. Nothing had come so close to imperial scope since the fall of the Roman Empire in the West. His great holdings were welded together mainly by the force of his own personality. During the early years of his reign he moved constantly from one area to another, "showing the flag" in a sense, and thus cementing the divergent parts together. In his later years he preferred to reside at Aachen with its warm springs and good hunting, but he continued to control his nobles by sending out *Missi* to instruct and inspect.

Charles was also a patron of the church and of the arts. He used military conquest at times as a means for the establishment of the church. The pattern of forced conversions, e.g. among the Saxons, was the rule, and dioceses were set up immediately after conquest.

When he began his rule, society in general, including the church and education, was at low ebb. He moved to reform various structures and thus initiated the so-called Carolingian Renaissance. Convinced that he was head of both church and state, he acted to improve the conditions within both, requiring church councils to act upon problems of clerical discipline, making the Rule of Chrodegang of Metz binding on the clergy, and supporting the monastic reforms of Benedict of Aniane (750-821).

He reached out to all of Europe to staff his educational ventures. Alcuin, Paul the Deacon, Einhard, and Theodolf, respectively English, Lombard, Frank, and Visigoth, answered his call to join the teaching program. The accomplishments of this renaissance are beyond the scope of this brief description. It is enough to note that they marked the end of the "Dark Ages." (See plate 10 for some of the early teaching leaders.)

In 800, in a ceremony still debated by scholars, Charles was formally crowned emperor by the Pope in Rome, thus constituting the Holy Roman Empire, an entity of tremendous force in the mind of Europe for generations, though more often figment than fact in actual power.

16

PLATE 6

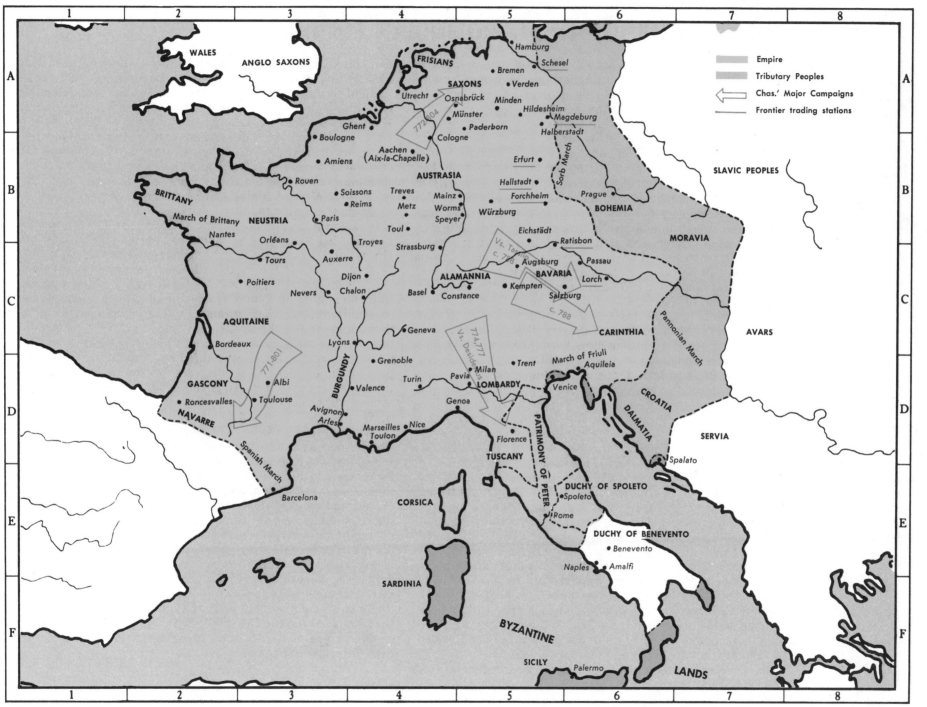

WALES

ANGLO SAXONS

FRISIANS

SAXONS
• Hamburg
• Schesel
• Bremen
• Verden
Utrecht • Osnabrück
• Minden
• Münster
• Hildesheim
• Paderborn • Magdeburg
Ghent • Cologne • Halberstadt
• Boulogne
Aachen
• Amiens (Aix-la-Chapelle)
AUSTRASIA
772-804

Erfurt

Sorb March

SLAVIC PEOPLES

BRITTANY
• Rouen
Treves Hallstadt •
• Soissons Mainz Forchheim
March of Brittany NEUSTRIA • Reims Metz Worms Prague
Nantes • Paris Toul Speyer Würzburg BOHEMIA
Orléans Troyes Strassburg Eichstädt MORAVIA
• Tours Auxerre Vs. Tassilo Ratisbon
• Dijon c. 796 Augsburg Passau
Poitiers Chalon ALAMANNIA Lorch
Nevers Basel BAVARIA
AQUITAINE Constance Kempten
Geneva Salzburg
Bordeaux Lyons c. 788 CARINTHIA AVARS
771-801 Grenoble Pannonian March
BURGUNDY Trent March of Friuli
GASCONY Albi Turin Milan Aquileia
Roncesvalles Valence Pavia Venice CROATIA
NAVARRE Avignon LOMBARDY DALMATIA
Arles Genoa SERVIA
Spanish March Marseilles Nice Florence PATRIMONY OF PETER
Toulon Spalato
Barcelona TUSCANY
774,777
Vs. Desiderius DUCHY OF SPOLETO
CORSICA Spoleto
Rome
DUCHY OF BENEVENTO
Benevento
SARDINIA Naples Amalfi

BYZANTINE

SICILY Palermo LANDS

Legend:
Empire
Tributary Peoples
Chas.' Major Campaigns
Frontier trading stations

17

PLATE 6

THE BREAKUP OF THE CAROLINGIAN EMPIRE

Ninth Century Warfare
From St. Gall Manuscript

Someone once asked, "What's in a name?" If one looks at the fate of the great empire of Charlemagne he would have to answer, "A great deal." The wide expanse of land and the diversities of many peoples had been held together by the strength and personal magnetism of the one man, Charles the Great. The names of some of his successors tell much of the story as to why the kingdom collapsed: Louis the Pious, sometimes called "the Debonair," Charles the Bald, Charles the Fat, and Charles the Simple.

Louis, the sole heir of Charles, could control neither the church, the empire, nor his own sons. While Charles had guided the church in innumerable ways, assuming that he was head of both church and state, acting to reform and even restructure when he felt it was necessary, Louis had none of the abilities of his father. Although Charles had been crowned emperor by Pope Leo in 800 he apparently wished to assert the independence of the secular crown as he had his son Louis crown himself in 813. This gesture of freedom was undone after Charles's death, as Louis characteristically allowed himself to be crowned again, this time by the church. The hands of Louis were certainly pious enough, they simply lacked the power and drive to lead. Only a very strong individual could maintain order in the widespread borders of the kingdom, and Louis was not such a person. An endless series of family quarrels turned into civil wars. Sons allied themselves against one another and against their father. The death of Louis (840) signaled the outbreak of fresh familial hostility, especially between Charles the Bald, Louis the German, and Lothair. A major battle near Auxerre in 841 saw the defeat of Lothair and his forces, but it was pyrrhic victory for Louis and Charles. The losses were so heavy on both sides as to bring into jeopardy the whole Carolingian dynasty's power to rule. Charles and Louis agreed not to make separate peace in the famous Oaths of Strassburg the next year, speaking in early French and German so that their troops could understand. The fragmentation of the empire was finalized by the Treaty of Verdun (843), according to which three sons (Louis, Charles, Lothair) each received a portion. The east went to Louis the German, the west to Charles the Bald, and the central area running from southern Italy to the coast of Frisia, was to be ruled by Lothair who also retained the imperial title.

The division that took place at Verdun is a part of the formative history of Germany and France. The central kingdom was naturally weak. It was completely artificial, had no natural defensible boundaries, and encompassed peoples of great diversity and no natural affinity. It was further weakened when, at Lothair's death (855), it was divided among his three sons. Their uncles, Charles and Louis, claimed the land, and at the Treaty of Mersen (870) the greater part of it was divided between them. This contested central area was to continue for centuries as an arena of war and a goal of conquest. The long-standing controversy between France and Germany over the territory of Alsace-Lorraine can be traced back to the treaties of Verdun and Mersen.

In addition to internal weakness the empire faced unremitting external pressure. The Viking forays had increased in intensity, and Normandy was permanently seized in 911. The Saracens raided in the south and even established permanent beachheads for inland sorties, striking at even the Alpine passes from their base at Garde Frainet. In the tenth century the Magyar horsemen swept through great parts of the old empire, thus adding to the chaos. Civil war, partition, raids, invasion—the society that first bloomed under Charles the Great trembled in such winds and gradually dried up. Feudalism, only one part of earlier social structure, now became its major mark. In the absence of central government, local lords had to assume responsibility for ruling and defense. The great empire of Charles the Great had fallen. Feudal chaos returned.

Theological discussion had begun and developed under Charles and his successors. Issues such as Adoptionist Christology, the Filioque addition to the Nicene Creed, and Iconoclasm were dealt with by Charles the Great and his court theologians. Later problems included Predestination, the Eucharist, and the Perpetual Virginity. While the discussions produced no original conclusions, but rather a reaffirmation of contemporary piety in each case, they do indicate that a renewed concern for theological matters was a part of this era. Figures like John Scotus Erigena, Rabanus Maurus, Paschasius Radbertus, Ratramnus, and Gottschalk are prominent in this story, but the final collapse of the empire also signaled the end of the intellectual ferment of the Carolingian Renaissance. England, under Alfred the Great (871-901), was the gathering place of the learned as the shadows of ignorance and chaos swept over the continent again.

PLATE 7

18

THE BREAKUP OF THE CAROLINGIAN EMPIRE

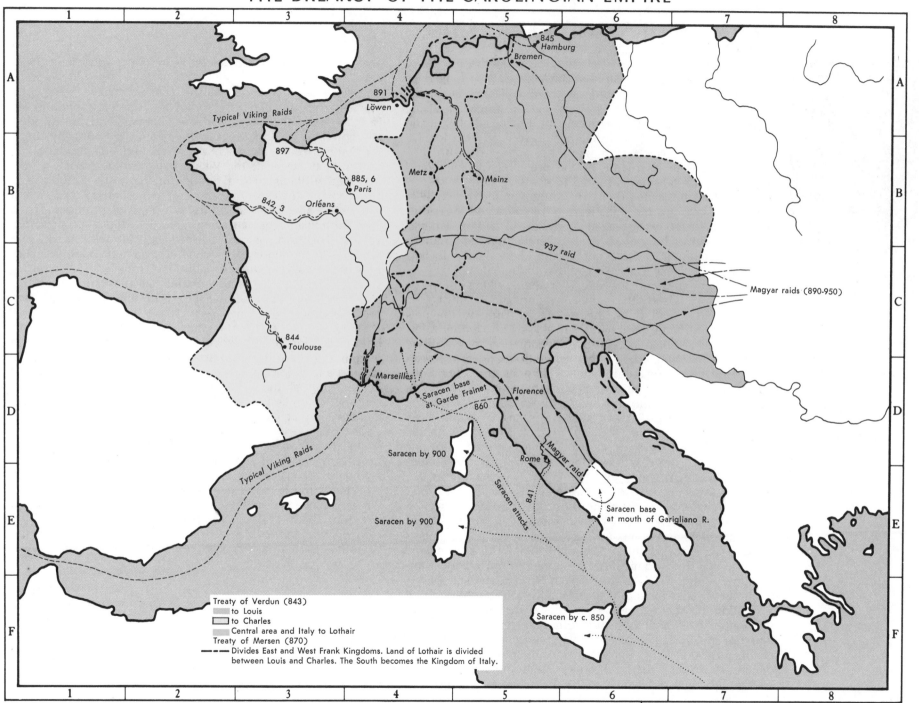

845 Hamburg
Bremen
891
Löwen
Typical Viking Raids
897
Metz
Mainz
885, 6
Paris
842, 3
Orléans
937 raid
Magyar raids (890-950)
844
Toulouse
Marseilles
Saracen base
at Garde Frainet
Florence
860
Typical Viking Raids
Saracen by 900
Magyar raid
Rome
841
Saracen attacks
Saracen base
at mouth of Gargliano R.
Saracen by 900
Saracen by c. 850

Treaty of Verdun (843)
   to Louis
   to Charles
   Central area and Italy to Lothair
Treaty of Mersen (870)
— · — · — Divides East and West Frank Kingdoms. Land of Lothair is divided
between Louis and Charles. The South becomes the Kingdom of Italy.

19

PLATE 7

VIKING RAIDS AND EXPANSION

Ninth Century Viking Carving

From the Oseberg finds

Often neglected, yet of vital significance in the history of Medieval Christianity, the story of the Vikings, their long ships and warlike, expansionist natures, deserves a place in our study.

Beginning in the age of Charlemagne the threat of Viking raids was a fact of life for Europe. The British scholar Alcuin could write, "We and our forefathers have lived here for 350 years, and never have terrors like these appeared in Britain." Driven from their own lands by the pressures of famine and population, the Northmen turned to the sea. Raids were carried out along the exposed coasts and then up the river valleys. On some occasions the ships were left behind and the sailors became horsemen who ravaged nearby towns and settlements. In 860 a fleet of long boats even entered the Mediterranean and pillaged along its coasts and up the Rhone Valley. In Italy not even the city of Florence could withstand them.

One might illustrate the effect of these Viking forays by reference to England. The earlier invaders and colonists, the Angles, Saxons, and Jutes, themselves fell prey to the new wave of warriors. In the last years of the eighth century a few Danish ships attacked in West Saxony and left a trail of blood and terror. In 790 another, larger expedition landed in Northumberland, storming Lindesfarne, killing its monks. By the following century the raids had become major invasions, and in the face of such pillage and murder the once bright flame of learning began to flicker and in some places to go out. Even the great school of York, that had produced men like Alcuin, was destroyed as were most of the other centers of learning in the north of the island kingdom, and in Ireland. An attendant decline in morality and church life is also noticeable. Only the great work of King Alfred of Wessex (d. 901) prevented far worse disaster as he drove off the Danes and also laid the groundwork for the development of an English nation.

A second phase of Viking expansion came as the raiders became settlers or colonists. Parts of Ireland, Frisia, and England came under their domination temporarily, and by 911 Normandy was theirs. These areas fell to Norwegians and Danes, while the Swedes looked to the east and managed to establish a kingdom in what is now Russia. They were known as Varangians after the "Vaerings"—the Nordic bodyguard of the great emperor in Constantinople. "Vaering," formerly meaning merchant, now stood for Viking warrior. Their expansionist tendencies even led them to attack Constantinople. Though beaten off, they did win lucrative commercial treaties. This group was gradually assimilated into the predominant Slavic race.

The primary Varangian motive seems to have been commercial. The valuable trade routes to Constantinople and the East lay along the Volga and the Dnieper, and the invaders attempted to control them. Settlements did spring up along the Dnieper route, e.g. at Ladoga, Kiev, and Novgorod.

The great extent of the Viking trade empire is seen in the imported artifacts of the period found in the Scandinavian homelands. Articles from as far east as Kashmir, Baghdad, and Samarkand have been found in Sweden. England, Ireland, and the Carolingian areas also contributed to the Viking treasure hoards. The invaders and traders also left their marks and products in the lands they visited. The famous marble lion of Athens carved with Runic inscriptions, the so-called Sword of St. Stephen, a tenth century Scandinavian weapon found in Prague, and the Viking burial ship of Brittany, all testify to the presence of the Northmen.

One effect of such action has already been noted in our brief discussion of the collapse of the Carolingian empire. In the ensuing chaos the Frankish church, deprived of its imperial support and guidance, turned more and more to the Bishop of Rome. Although the Gallicanism of a Hincmar of Reims (ninth century) would continue to be a factor for centuries, the Ultramontanism that eventually triumphed received firm and increasing support.

One could point to a third phase in the history of Viking expansion. Some of the areas settled by Northmen, notably Normandy, later sent out expeditions of note. In this category one marks the invasion of England in 1066, of South Italy in the early eleventh century with the establishment of a Norman Kingdom there (1030-1190), and also the founding of the Norman Kingdom of Antioch in 1098 in connection with the Crusades.

*From the fury of
the Northmen,
good Lord, deliver us.*
Medieval Prayer

PLATE 8

VIKING RAIDS AND EXPANSION

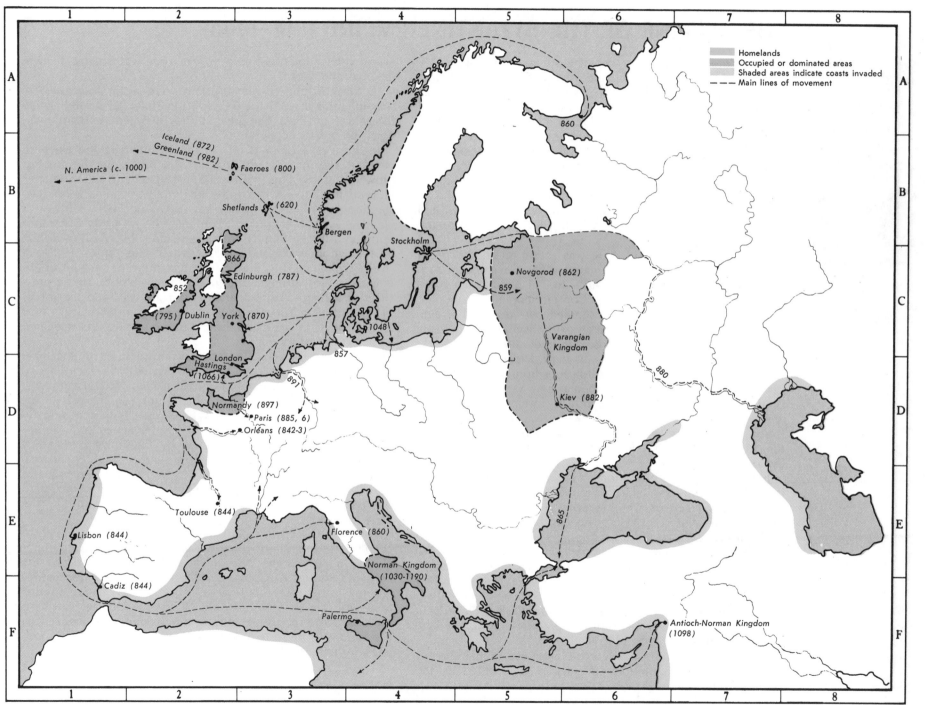

Homelands
Occupied or dominated areas
Shaded areas indicate coasts invaded
- - - - Main lines of movement

Iceland (872)
Greenland (982)
N. America (c. 1000)
Faeroes (800)
Shetlands (620)
Bergen
Stockholm
860
Novgorod (862)
859
Varangian Kingdom
880
Kiev (882)
866
852
Edinburgh (787)
(795) Dublin
York (870)
1048
857
891
London
Hastings (1066)
Normandy (897)
Paris (885, 6)
Orléans (842-3)
865
Toulouse (844)
Lisbon (844)
Florence (860)
Norman Kingdom (1030-1190)
Cadiz (844)
Palermo
Antioch-Norman Kingdom (1098)

PLATE 8

THE DECLINE OF THE BYZANTINE EMPIRE (814-1355)

The Virgin and Child

From Sancta Sophia, Constantinople

After a momentary return to past glory under Justinian (527-65) around two-thirds of the land area of the empire was lost in the first surge of Arab military expansion. Two factors contributed to this successful Arab onrush. First, the Persian and Byzantine empires had weakened each other so much by their own conflict as to be unable to counter a new opponent effectively, and second, the heretical Monophysite Christians in the east, long persecuted by the Byzantine church, often looked on the Arabs as liberators rather than enemies to be opposed. Even Constantinople was attacked in 673 and 717, but survived, protected by its great walls, water defenses, and the newly invented Greek Fire which destroyed much of the Arab fleet.

During this same period there was action on another front as the Bulgarians, having subjugated other Slavic peoples in the Balkans, began to move south. In 711 a Bulgarian force actually attacked the suburbs of Constantinople.

The earlier days of weakness seemed over during the reign of Leo III (the Isaurian). Despite an extremely bitter and costly struggle over the use of icons, Leo did raise the siege of Constantinople and push the Arabs back. His son Constantine V (741-75) drove the invaders still farther from the walls of the capital and fought in Syria, Armenia, and Mesopotamia. The Isaurian Dynasty (717-802) was not as fortunate in the west where both Rome and Exarchate were lost. Much of the lost territory in the east was regained by the end of the tenth century as Crete, Antioch, and North Syria again came under the Byzantine throne.

In this same period both Moravia and Bohemia were missionized. Work among the Bulgars was initiated, probably by Christian captives taken from Adrianople (813) by the victorious Bulgars. Boris, the Bulgar king, was baptized in 864 and, after some hesitation, cast his lot with Constantinople rather than Rome. The most famous missionaries to the Slavs were the brothers Cyril (d. 869) and Methodius (d. 885) who arrived in Moravia in 864. From Moravia the Christian message reached Bohemia in the ninth century.

The height of power was reached under Basil II (976-1025), in whose reign there was mission expansion among the Russians (Vladimir was baptized in 988).

The eleventh century marked the beginning of the end for the eastern empire. Internal dissension contributed as the landed aristocracy fought the imperial office-holders for power at the very moment when a united force was needed to face external attackers.

In the east the forces of Islam were again increasing in strength, and in 1071 the Seljuk Turks defeated the Byzantine forces at Manzikert. The great source of Byzantine manpower, Asia Minor, was now lost.

In the west Sicily was lost to the Normans in the eleventh century, and in the early years of the thirteenth the greatest blow fell as the Fourth Crusade, urged on by the Venetians, ignored the papal command and turned to the sack of Constantinople. A Latin Kingdom was established with Baldwin of Flanders as emperor; a Latin Patriarch was set up in Constantinople and the Eastern Church was made subservient to Rome. This kingdom collapsed in 1261 when the capital fell to a rival Greek state, but the revived Byzantine empire never recovered its lost strength and gradually succumbed to the pressures of Serbians and Bulgarians from the west and the forces of the Ottoman Turks from the east. Constantinople fell, after a bitter siege, in 1453, and the Byzantine empire was relegated to books of history.

The Eastern Church during the period pictured by the plate was characterized by its patriarchal system in which several main cities led, with Constantinople having general authority. This meant freedom on the one hand, but also chaos at times, in that there was no unified way to deal with the heresies that plagued certain patriarchates, e.g. Jerusalem and Alexandria. The church was also marked by Caesaropapism, i.e. it was under the domination of the emperor. This dependence upon and obedience to the crown were in marked contrast to the situation in the West where the bishops of Rome often operated in what amounted to a political vacuum during the early Middle Ages.

A long series of political and theological conflicts dating to even before the rule of Gregory I in the West came to a minor climax in 863 when Pope Nicholas I (858-67) declared the Patriarch Photius of Constantinople deposed. The decree was ignored in the East. The final act came in 1054 in the conflict between Leo IX (1049-54) and Patriarch Michael Cerularis (1043-58). The schism, so long in the making, was finalized by the actions of these two. Only in recent years has this breach been formally bridged.

PLATE 9

THE DECLINE OF THE BYZANTINE EMPIRE (814-1355)

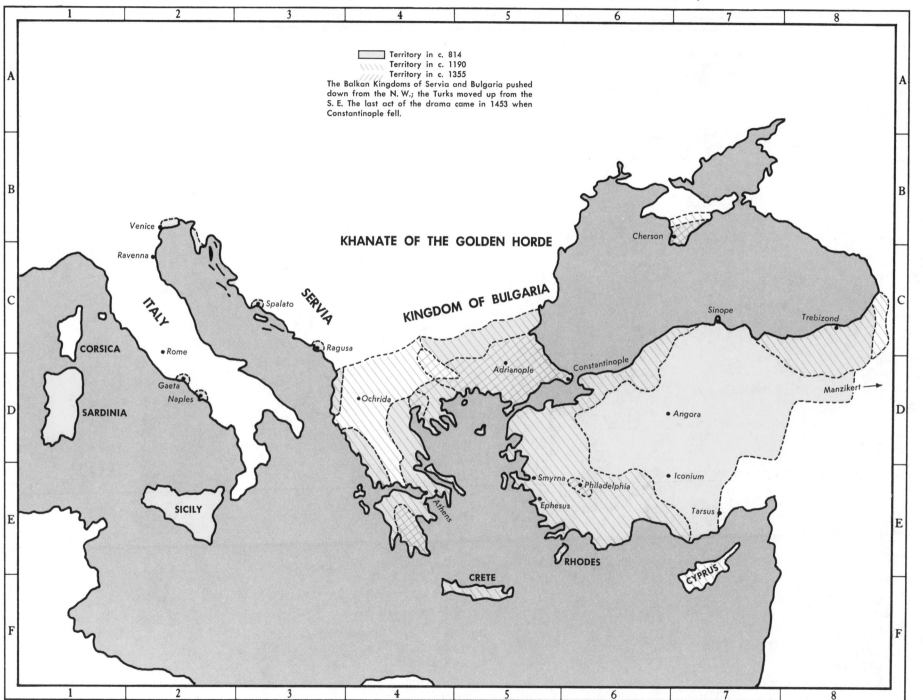

Territory in c. 814
Territory in c. 1190
Territory in c. 1355
The Balkan Kingdoms of Servia and Bulgaria pushed down from the N. W.; the Turks moved up from the S. E. The last act of the drama came in 1453 when Constantinople fell.

KHANATE OF THE GOLDEN HORDE

Cherson

Venice

Ravenna

ITALY

SERVIA

KINGDOM OF BULGARIA

Sinope

Trebizond

Spalato

CORSICA

Rome

Ragusa

Adrianople

Constantinople

Manzikert →

Gaeta

Ochrida

Angora

Naples

SARDINIA

Iconium

Smyrna

Philadelphia

Tarsus

SICILY

Athens

Ephesus

RHODES

CRETE

CYPRUS

F   23

PLATE 9

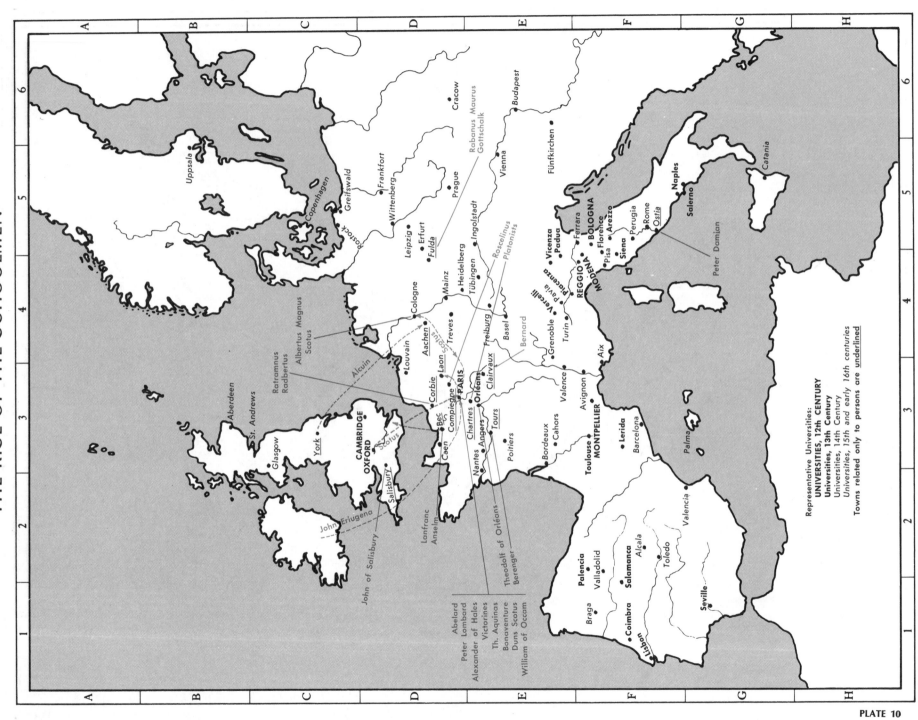

THE RISE OF THE SCHOOLMEN

Uppsala

Copenhagen

Greifswald

Rostock

Frankfort

Wittenberg

Cracow

Prague

Leipzig

Erfurt

Fulda

Rabanus Maurus
Gottschalk

Vienna

Budapest

Fünfkirchen

Heidelberg

Ingolstadt

Tübingen

Roscelinus
Platonists

Vicenza

Padua

Ferrara

BOLOGNA

Florence

Pavia

Pisa

Arezzo

Siena

Perugia

Rome

Ostia

Naples

Salerno

Peter Damian

Catania

Mainz

Cologne

Aachen

Albertus Magnus
Scotus

Treves

Freiburg

Basel

Clairvaux

Bernard

Vercelli

Piacenza

REGGIO

MODENA

Grenoble

Turin

Louvain

Laon

Corbie

Compiegne

PARIS

Orléans

Ratramnus
Radbertus

Alcuin

Scotus

Aberdeen

St. Andrews

Glasgow

York

Scotus

CAMBRIDGE
OXFORD

Bec

Anselm

Lanfranc

Caen

Chartres

Angers

Nantes

Tours

Poitiers

Bordeaux

Cahors

Valence

Avignon

Aix

Salisbury

John of Salisbury

John Eriugena

Theodolf of Orléans

Berenger

Abelard
Peter Lombard
Alexander of Hales
Victorines
Th. Aquinas
Bonaventure
Duns Scotus
William of Occam

Toulouse

MONTPELLIER

Lerida

Barcelona

Palma

Valencia

Palencia

Valladolid

Alcala

Salamanca

Toledo

Braga

Coimbra

Lisbon

Seville

Representative Universities:
UNIVERSITIES, 12th CENTURY
Universities, 13th Century
Universities, 14th Century
Universities, 15th and early 16th centuries
Towns related only to persons are underlined

PLATE 10

THE RISE OF THE SCHOOLMEN

Those who would dismiss medieval times as "the dark ages" have not paid close enough attention to the real intellectual ferment that characterized the period, or at least parts of it. Important centers of learning grew up in connection with monastic houses and cathedrals where the heritage of the past was carefully nurtured and passed on to succeeding generations. Men like the Venerable Bede (d. 735) in Northumbria kept the light burning, and when Charles the Great came to the throne of the Franks (771) he consciously embarked on an educational program for his empire, importing scholars such as Alcuin for this purpose.

There were theological stirrings in the Carolingian era. The earlier years of mission warfare were passed and with the advent of time for reflection men like Radbertus, Ratramnus, Rabanus Maurus, Gottschalk, and others took up the task of theological formulation and clarification. Most of the early leaders were monastics, but later some, notably Abelard, were connected with cathedral schools. Abelard also serves as a linking figure between cathedral school and university.

Students flocked to centers of learning from all parts of Europe. Bologna was noted as a center for the study of law, Paris and Oxford for theology, Salerno for medicine. In places like these a change took place in that students and teachers banded together, much in the same way as the guilds had done, for mutual protection and for order. The associations thus formed also sought more effective management for student life and also better means of regulating admission into the teaching profession. This banding together eventuated in the founding of the "universitas scholarium," i.e. the university of scholars. The precise dating of the earliest of these universities is impossible, although the year 1200 is generally accepted.

It was at the universities that the great schoolmen or "scholastics" flourished. The greatest of the scholastics were members of the Mendicant Orders, i.e. the Dominicans and the Franciscans. The names of Albertus Magnus and Thomas Aquinas give honor to the Dominicans, while Alexander of Hales, Bonaventura, Duns Scotus, and William of Occam bear the Franciscan banner. Just as the church was central in all of society, so also theology was the queen of the sciences, and the brightest jewels in her crown were men like Aquinas and Bonaventura.

PLATE 10

ITALY AND TWO GREAT POPES:
Gregory I and Innocent III

We have already referred to the tumultuous times of Gregory I. This plate (11) shows in some detail the Italy of his day. Its division between the Eastern Empire and the Lombards is plain. The real power of the peninsula is not evident from a glance at a map, however. The Emperor, occupied in Constantinople, ruled only in name through his Exarch, who rested safely in Ravenna. The only force to halt the tide of the onrushing Lombards was the Pope himself. Gregory's firmness and astuteness enhanced his own power and defended and gained prestige for the church at the same moment. The collapse of imperial power in the west also cast him into the role of provider for the hungry masses. The machinery of the church and its large holdings of land were turned to this task.

Times and maps had changed by the time of Innocent III (1198-1216). What other popes had claimed, Innocent did. He ruled Europe. By 1208 he was lord of Italy, having extended the papal lands, made Tuscany a feudal fief in the north, allied himself with the commercial cities of the north, and controlled the factions in Rome. The Pope, for the moment, was blessed with a secure base of power in Italy.

Although the Normans controlled the south, Innocent was the power behind the throne in the Empire; Frederick II was his man, really the creature of papal power. In France Philip II had bowed to Innocent in the matter of a contested wedding. Philip had repudiated his bride of one day and had this act approved by his bishops. Innocent, responding to the appeal of the wife, placed France under the Interdict (1201) and encouraged England to take up arms against its cross-channel foe. This pressure forced a grudging royal reunion.

In England the controversy centered on the appointment of the new Archbishop of Canterbury. King John's threats and appropriation of church property were countered by the Interdict, personal excommunication, a papal announcement freeing all from any oaths made to John, and finally, a papal encouragement to France to invade the island kingdom. The obstreperous king was beaten. Portugal and Aragon also were fiefs owing allegiance to the see of Peter.

This pontificate marks the peak of papal power. Within one hundred years much of this secular authority had slipped away as new forces, e.g. national spirit, enabled powerful rulers such as Philip the Fair of France and Edward I of England to defy Pope Boniface VIII (1294-1303).

PLATES 11 and 12

Master and Students
Albrecht Dürer, c. 1490

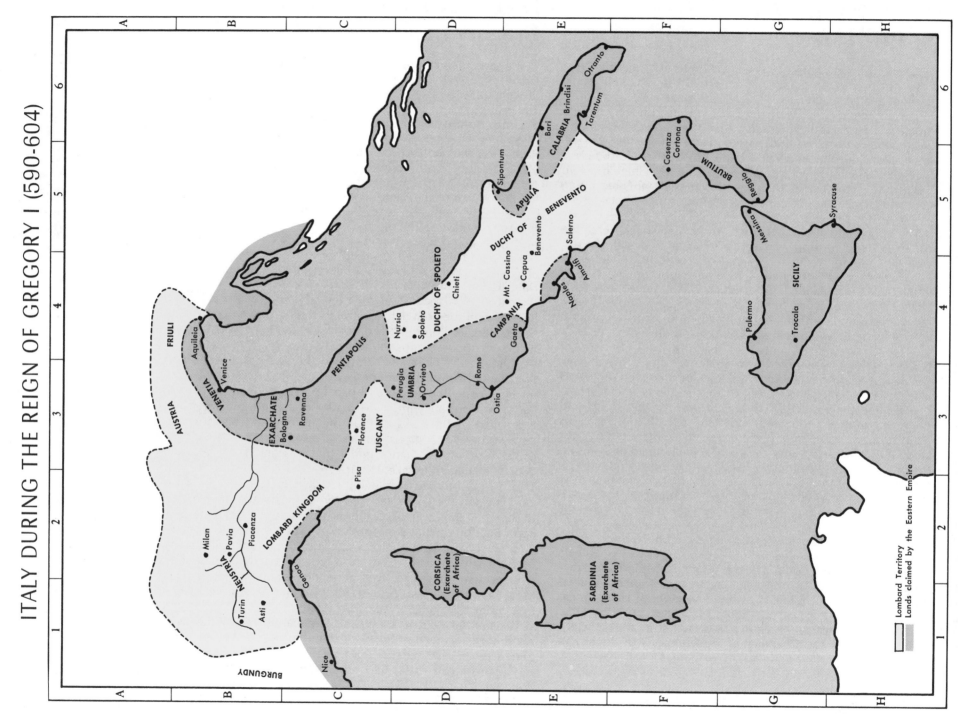

ITALY DURING THE REIGN OF GREGORY I (590-604)

AUSTRIA

FRIULI

Aquileia

VENETIA

Venice

EXARCHATE

Bologna • Ravenna

PENTAPOLIS

NEUSTRIA

Milan •
Pavia •
Piacenza •

Turin •
Asti •

LOMBARD KINGDOM

Genoa •

Pisa •

Florence •

TUSCANY

Nice •

BURGUNDY

Nursia •
Spoleto •

DUCHY OF SPOLETO

Chieti •

Perugia •
Orvieto •

UMBRIA

Rome •

Ostia •

Gaeta •

CAMPANIA

Mt. Cassino • Capua •

Benevento •

Naples •

Amalfi •

Salerno •

DUCHY OF BENEVENTO

Sipontum •

APULIA

Bari •

Brindisi

Tarentum •

Otranto

CALABRIA

BRUTTIUM

Cosenza •
Cortona •

Reggio •

Messina •

SICILY

Palermo •

Trocala •

Syracuse •

CORSICA
(Exarchate
of Africa)

SARDINIA
(Exarchate
of Africa)

Lombard Territory
Lands claimed by the Eastern Empire

PLATE 11

A B C D E F G H

6

Brindisi
Otranto

5

Siponto
Trani
Bari
Acerenza
Matera
Taranto

NORMAN KINGDOM

Capua · Benevento
Naples
Amalfi
Conza
Salerno
Sorrento
Rossano
Cosenza

Reggio

4

Udine
Aquileia
Grado
Venice

MARCH OF TREVISO

MARCH
of ANCONA

D. of SPOLETO

PATRIMONY
OF PETER

Rome

SICILY

Messina

Syracuse

3

Ravenna

ROMANIOLA

LANDS
OF MATHILDA

Florence

TUSCANY

Palermo

Monreale

2

Milan · LOMBARDY
Pavia
Piacenza
Pisa

Genoa

CORSICA
(to Pisa,
1090)

SARDINIA
(to Pisa,
11th cent.)

Sassari
Oristano
Cagliari

1

Turin
Asti

PIEDMONT

Nice

27

A B C D E F G H

Claimed by Emperor
Papal States
Lands claimed by the Papacy
Norman Kingdom of Sicily; Hohenstauffen
land ff. 1189
Towns in italics: Archbishoprics

PLATE 12

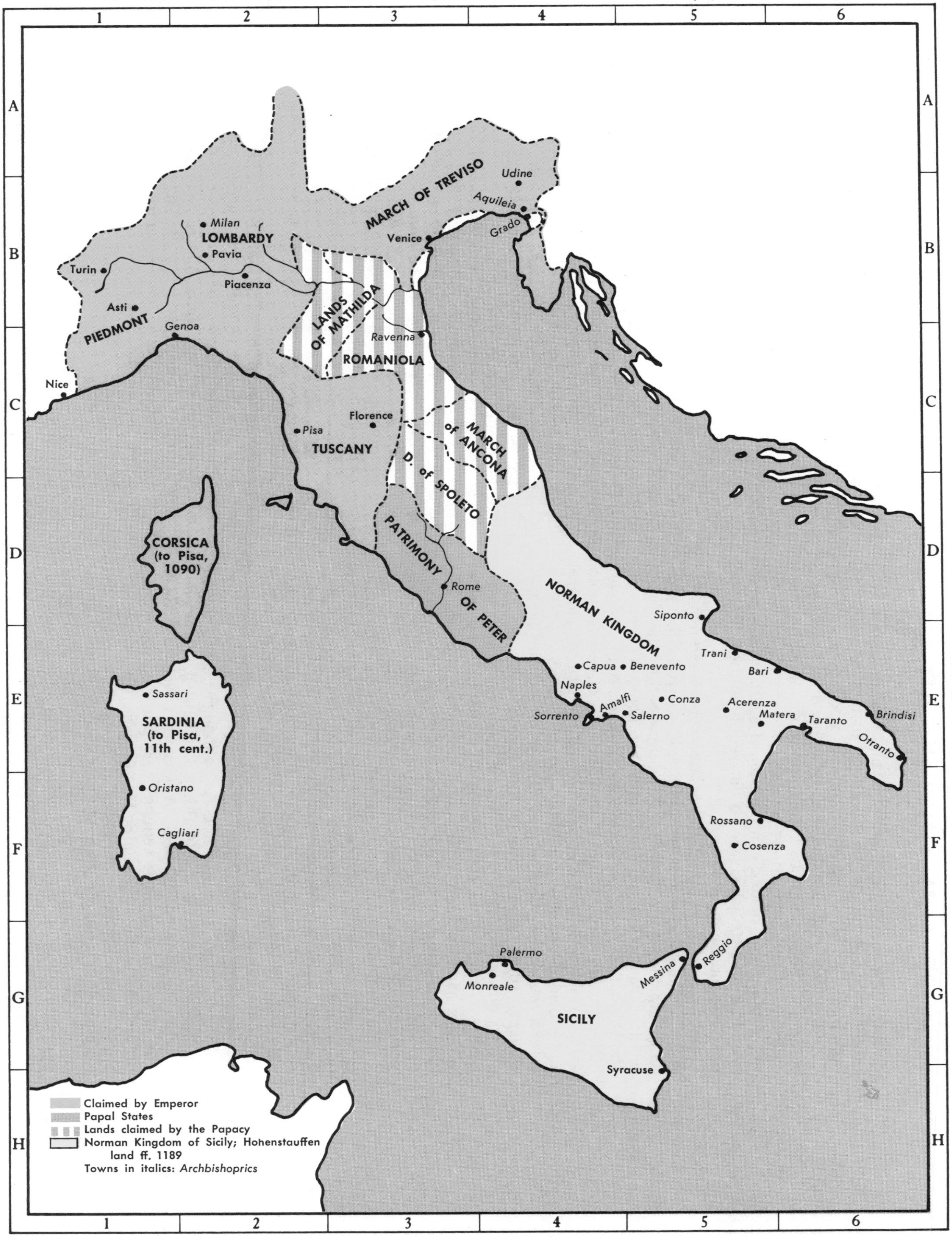

EUROPE AND THE CRUSADES

The Christian Warrior
From an old engraving

From 1095 to 1270 the attention of Christian Europe was fixed on the East and on the convulsive attempts to wrest the holy places from the Infidel. Thousands upon thousands set out under the cross. The flower of knighthood marched away, as did the dregs of society. Even children attempted the road to the Holy Sepulcher. They marched away, to spend themselves and return, or to die in a welter of blood, or of plague or of thirst in a sunbaked land so different from the greenness of France and Germany.

One must ask what caused this politico-military and religious spasm in the body of Western Christendom. Two Eastern emperors (Michael VII and Alexius I), hard pressed by the forces of Islam, had sent requests for aid to two popes (Gregory VII and Urban II). Their opponents were not Arabs, but Turks who had been converted to Islam by the Samanids of Persia. While earlier Mohammedan forces had allowed Christian pilgrimage and provided a relatively stable government, the Seljuk Turks were a brutal and intolerant people who preyed on Christian travelers, killing or selling them into slavery, and who desecrated the holy places. The news of this treatment aroused Europe as much as the calls for help from the Eastern empire.

There had also been some notable recent successes in the fight against Islam. Sicily and parts of Spain had been reconquered, and there was a conviction that the time had come to turn back the infidel tide in other lands as well.

One must also note the deepened religious feelings in Europe at this time which manifested itself in various reform movements and in the desire for pilgrimage. When one couples this with economic privation on the continent, the existence of a class that lived to do battle, and the hope of gain, either temporal or eternal, by taking the cross one has at least a partial background picture.

Gregory VII, enmeshed in the Investiture Controversy, was unable to go to the aid of the East although he had hoped to lead an army himself, but Urban II (1088-99) did act decisively. At Clermont in 1095, in what may well have been one of the most effective sermons ever preached, he roused the French nobility to go on the First Crusade. He pictured the beauties of Jerusalem, "the navel of the world," and of the Holy Land. "The way is short," he said (one suspects he knew rather little about geography), "the toil will be followed by an incorruptible crown." The horrors of infidel occupation were stressed and contrasted with the valor of the French no-

bility until finally, in a great outburst, the hearers responded, "On to Jerusalem, Deus vult." The cross was taken as a sign of their pledge to go. In the excess of the moment some were even reported to have branded themselves with this symbol when crimson cloth for making more conventional designs ran out.

Other contingents, more mobs than armies, also set out, plundering and burning Jewish communities en route. Part of this rabble reached Constantinople, crossed into enemy territory, and was completely destroyed before the armies of the princes even arrived.

The Crusade of the Princes had as much confusion and difficulty, but more success. Nicea fell to them in June 1097, next Dorylaeum, Edessa, and finally, after a bitter siege, Antioch in June of 1098. One year later they arrived at Jerusalem and conquered it, bathing the city in the blood of thousands of its Jewish and Mohammedan inhabitants. A Latin Kingdom was established in 1100 which lasted until 1187 when Saladin reconquered the area, thus triggering demands in Europe for another crusade (the Third).

Other expeditions followed, most of which were dismal failures. One, the Fourth, did not even make it to the Holy Land, but turned aside on Venetian insistence and plundered the city of Constantinople, the last bastion of the Eastern Empire (see plates 9 and 13). Many of the treasures found in Venice today are of Eastern origin and have come by way of the plunderers of the Fourth Crusade.

Methods of numbering the crusades vary greatly. Whether there were six, seven, or twelve need not concern us. The last great effort was mounted by Louis the Saint, of France, in 1270. His death at Tunis marks the end of an era.

The crusades failed in their three goals of freeing the Holy Land, reuniting East and West, and halting the advance of Islam. Among the effects of the effort were the bringing of Arabic knowledge to the West, an increase of trade and, oddly, in the prestige of the papacy, and the growth in the West of Eastern varieties of heresy, e.g. the Manichaean, which eventuated in the rise of the Cathari in southern France.

PLATE 13

EUROPE AND THE CRUSADES

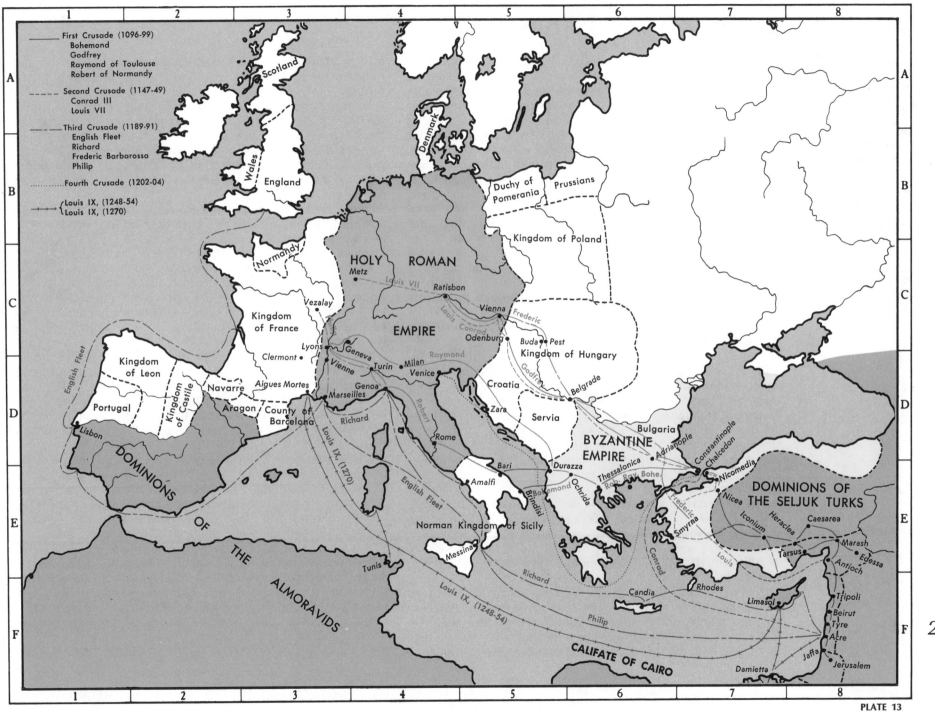

First Crusade (1096-99)
Bohemond
Godfrey
Raymond of Toulouse
Robert of Normandy

Second Crusade (1147-49)
Conrad III
Louis VII

Third Crusade (1189-91)
English Fleet
Richard
Frederic Barbarossa
Philip

Fourth Crusade (1202-04)

Louis IX, (1248-54)
Louis IX, (1270)

Scotland

England

Wales

Denmark

Normandy

HOLY ROMAN

Metz

Vezelay

Kingdom
of France

Lyons

Clermont

Geneva

Vienne

Turin

Milan

Venice

Aigues Mortes

Genoa

Marseilles

County of
Barcelona

Aragon

Navarre

Kingdom
of Leon

Kingdom
of Castile

Portugal

Lisbon

DOMINIONS

OF

THE

ALMORAVIDS

Louis VII

Ratisbon

Vienna

Frederic

Odenburg

EMPIRE

Raymond

Buda

Pest

Kingdom of Hungary

Croatia

Zara

Servia

Belgrade

Duchy of
Pomerania

Prussians

Kingdom of Poland

Bulgaria

Adrianople

Durazza

Thessalonica

Ochrida

Bohemond

Rob. Ray. Bohe.

Constantinople

Chalcedon

Nicomedia

Nicea

DOMINIONS OF
THE SELJUK TURKS

Smyrna

Frederic

Louis

Conrad

Iconium

Heraclea

Caesarea

Tarsus

Marash

Edessa

Antioch

Tripoli

Beirut

Tyre

Acre

Jaffa

Jerusalem

Rome

Bari

Amalfi

Brindisi

Norman Kingdom of Sicily

Messina

Tunis

English Fleet

Richard

Louis IX, (1270)

Louis IX, (1248-54)

Richard

Philip

Candia

Rhodes

Limasol

Damietta

BYZANTINE
EMPIRE

English Fleet

CALIFATE OF CAIRO

29

PLATE 13

MEDIEVAL MONASTICISM

The Monk at Work

From Dürer's Illustrations to the Revelations of St. Bridget

It would be hard to overestimate the influence of monasticism on the medieval community and church. The monks were the builders of civilization. They educated nations, preserving and passing on the heritage of antiquity while the currents of ignorance swirled around outside their walls. They drained the swamps, farmed, and taught others the skills needed not only for survival but also for growth into a more cultured age.

The monks were also the great builders of the church. They saw themselves as representing the church and exerted themselves through missions and reform. The great missionary and reformer Boniface (d. 754) exemplifies this theme. There were moments, some of them rather lengthy, of corruption, but there was also a persistent impulse to reform, to return to the purity of the monastic rule.

The ideal of withdrawal from the world in order to serve God better, and in some instances also the world, began in the East but was an early Western import through the efforts of men like Jerome, Ambrose, and Augustine. Martin of Tours and Vincent of Lerins are towering early figures in the European expression of monasticism.

The Benedictines are basic to our story. Founded in the early years of the sixth century as a reform and unifying movement within current monasticism, the group took the rule composed by Benedict of Nursia (529) as its guide. This famous statement maintains its central significance to this day. It stipulated that the irrevocable vows of poverty, chastity, and obedience were to be taken after a year of testing. Life was organized around the two poles of prayer and labor. Fixed times within each day were given over to services of worship, or the so-called canonical hours. In the early spring, for example, the order of the day would run as follows: Vigils at about 2:00 a.m., Lauds at 4:30 a.m., Prime at 6:00 a.m., Terce at 9:00 a.m., Sext at 12 noon, None at 4:00 p.m., Vespers at 4:30 p.m., Collation at 5:45 p.m., and Compline at 6:00 p.m. The monks worked at other times, according to their abilities and the instructions of their leader or abbot.

This rule spread slowly, but by the time of Charles the Great it was basic in the West. It maintained its normative character through much of the Middle Ages. A competitor was the Celtic variety which left its mark in a mission fervor that spread to the continent and in an extremely rigorist view of religion. (See plate 3.)

The chaos following the Carolingian collapse affected monasticism. The great task of restoring the moral, intellectual, and religious life of the West began in the movements of monastic reform.

A prime example of such an endeavor is that of Cluny. Founded in 910 in Burgundy, this group fought against impurity within the church and also against lay control. When the impulse to change originated at Cluny united with the papacy significant changes took place. Several of the popes were themselves Cluniacs. Gregory VII (d. 1085) is the most prominent example.

The ascetic ideal found expression elsewhere in the tenth and eleventh centuries. In the north Gerhard of Brogne (d. 959) and in the south Romuald of Ravenna (d. 1027) and Peter Damiani (d. 1072) moved to positions of leadership.

Cluny became wealthy and corrupt and another movement, the Cistercians, reacted to them. In 1098 the Cistercian founder, Robert of Dijon, began work at Citeaux, attempting to return to the earlier Benedictine ideal, largely abandoned by the Cluniacs. The new order flourished. Its most famous member was Bernard of Clairvaux (d. 1153).

One should also briefly note the rise of military orders in connection with the crusades. The Knights of St. John, or Hospitallars, were established in 1110 and their rivals, the Templars, in 1118. They were protectors of pilgrims and of the holy places. The most powerful of such orders came to be the Teutonic Knights. There were others, but not as significant as these.

In the thirteenth century a new type, the mendicant, who was a monastic *in* the world, appeared in the work of Francis of Assisi and Dominic. They reacted to the now-wealthy and lax Cistercians and advocated a return to the ideal of apostolic poverty. Most of the great teachers of the thirteenth century, e.g. Thomas Aquinas and Bonaventura, were Mendicants.

It is not necessary to catalog the multitude of orders and houses present in the Middle Ages. For example, in the twelfth century there were nearly 1,500 Cluniac houses, and in the thirteenth, the Cistercian had 742 houses plus around 900 nunneries. The plate attempts only to show representative centers significant as to date, prominent leaders, mother houses, and locations of reform.

30

PLATE 14

MEDIEVAL MONASTICISM

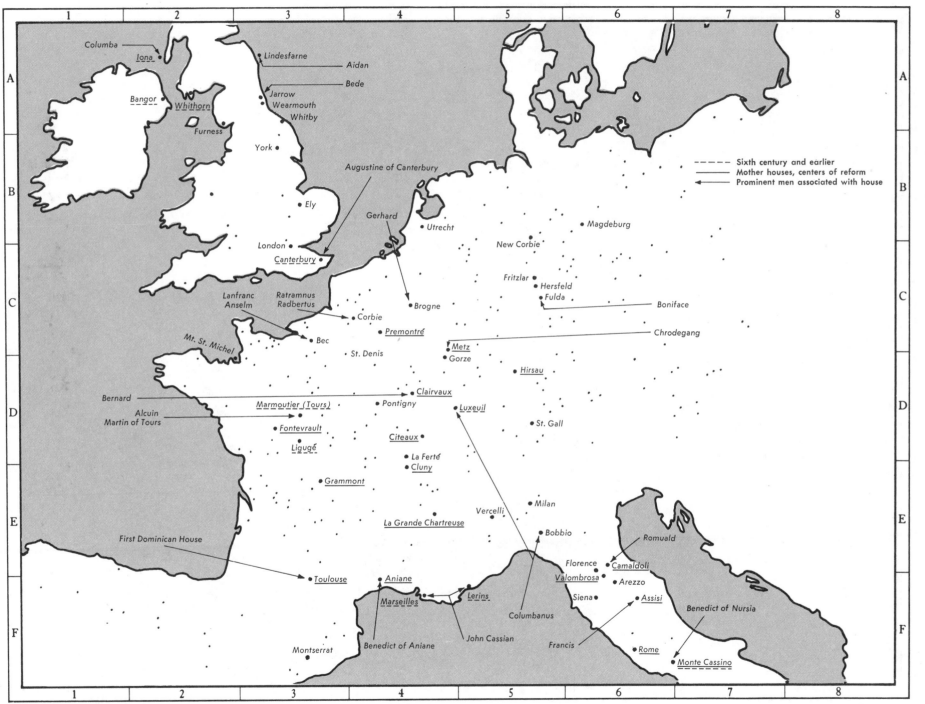

Columba → *Iona*
Lindesfarne → Aidan
→ Bede
Bangor *Whithorn* Jarrow
Wearmouth
Whitby
Furness
York
Augustine of Canterbury
Gerhard
Ely
London
Utrecht *Magdeburg*
New Corbie
Canterbury
Fritzlar
Hersfeld
Fulda → Boniface
Lanfranc Ratramnus
Anselm Radbertus → Corbie *Brogne*
Mt. St. Michel *Premontré* Chrodegang
Bec *Metz*
St. Denis Gorze
Hirsau
Bernard → *Clairvaux*
Alcuin *Marmoutier (Tours)* *Pontigny* *Luxeuil*
Martin of Tours *St. Gall*
Fontevrault
Citeaux
Ligugé *La Ferté*
Cluny
Grammont
Milan
Vercelli
La Grande Chartreuse
First Dominican House *Bobbio*
Romuald
Florence *Camaldoli*
→ *Toulouse* *Valombrosa* *Arezzo*
Aniane Siena *Assisi*
Marseilles *Lerins* Benedict of Nursia
Columbanus Francis → *Rome*
Montserrat Benedict of Aniane John Cassian *Monte Cassino*

- - - - Sixth century and earlier
———— Mother houses, centers of reform
⟵——— Prominent men associated with house

31

PLATE 14

MEDIEVAL COMMERCE AND INDUSTRY

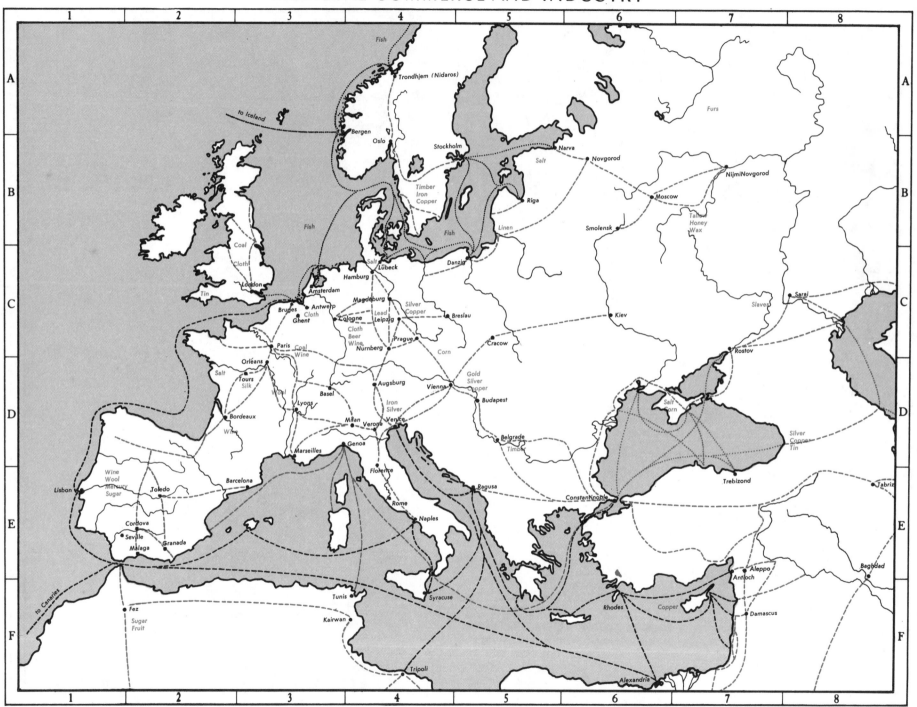

32

----- Major overland routes ········· Sea Routes ----- Sea Routes, Genoa - - - Sea Routes, Venice ·········· Sea Routes, Hanseatic League

PLATE 15

MEDIEVAL COMMERCE AND INDUSTRY

Very few of the people in any period are bishops and archbishops, monks or nuns, generals or emperors. The great mass of medieval population worked on the soil, or, as trade developed, in commercial cities. One of the great factors leading to the decline in authority of both Empire and Papacy was, in fact, the rise of a wealthy middle class which was dependent upon trade. New and seemingly uncontrollable winds swept the continent as the old agricultural economy turned in part to other areas of endeavor, and as the system of barter was replaced by an infant capitalism in the late years of the Middle Ages.

The routes by which trade products traveled are important in that ideas spread along the same lines of communication, and the commercial cities also became centers for learning and the dissemination of new ideas. Count the number of sea and overland routes that converge on Constantinople and you will have some understanding of her wealth and prestige. Our plate indicates major overland and sea routes. One must not forget the river systems as mercantile arteries.

The Vikings were among the great traders of the early Middle Ages, although they often preferred slaughter to salesmanship. They transported English wool to the Flemish, and brought amber, furs, slaves, tallow, and honey from the East. (See plate 8 for the Viking movement.) The only trade town of significance that developed in this early era was Venice. Blessed with an unsurpassed location for both sea and overland shipment, Venice took over the routes of the crumbling Byzantine empire and prospered.

By the thirteenth century new leaders had appeared. In the north the Flemish busied themselves in the cloth and carrying trades and also reached into the Baltic via Lübeck to compete with the Russians, Danes, and Germans. By the end of the century they had been excluded from this area by the Germans. To the south a rival for Venice had risen in Genoa. The bills of lading of the competitors indicate that they carried mainly wool, metals, timber, and timber products to the East, and brought back textiles, fruits, and most important, spices.

Great mercantile empires developed. One example is the Hanseatic League which in the thirteenth and fourteenth centuries was the chief commercial actor in a vast area stretching from Bergen to Leipzig, north and south, and from Novgorod to London, east to west. Similar empires were created by the competitors, Venice and Genoa. **PLATE 15**

THE GREAT SCHISM (1378-1417)

New currents were coursing through Europe in the fourteenth century. The rise of national consciousness and the appearance of independent groups, e.g. a wealthy middle class, were among the most significant. The days of absolute papal supremacy were past. Boniface VIII (d. 1303) illustrates this decline. Unable to recognize the changed situation, he tried to rule in the grand manner of Innocent III (d. 1216). The kings of England and France defied him; Philip of France even came south and imprisoned the Pope. *Sic transit gloria mundi.* Thus began a period of complete French domination of the papal throne. The triumph was complete when the papal residence and court moved to Avignon and remained there through seven popes (1309-77).

In 1377, after nearly seventy years in Avignon, the papacy returned to Rome. The following year the Pope, Gregory XI, died and the cardinals, under pressure of the Roman populace, elected an Italian as Urban VI. The French cardinals, alienated by Urban, withdrew from Rome and proceeded to elect another pope, Clement VII, claiming the first election had been under duress and so invalid. There were now two popes, one in Rome, one in Avignon. The Roman pope, Urban VI, appointed a new college of cardinals and the schism seemed final.

The tragic confusion of the period is hard to imagine: two supreme pontiffs claiming allegiance of the faithful, anathematizing each other. Europe was divided between the two. Our plate indicates the shape of this division.

Out of this confusion the Conciliar Movement was born. Men like Dante, Marsilius of Padua, and William of Occam began calling for a council of the church. Ecclesiastical government would be in council hands, rather than papal. Others took up the cry and finally, in 1409, a council was called to meet at Pisa which was to end the schism and reform the church. Unfortunately the two papal incumbents refused to be deposed, and so the pope elected by Pisa (Alexander V) became, not a healing figure, but rather merely one of three popes. This intolerable situation was corrected at the Council of Constance in 1417 when all three pontiffs were declared deposed and a new pope, Martin V, elected. The councils had healed the schism, but in so doing had lost their claim to govern the church. Papal hands again grasped the reins, although the conciliar idea persisted well into the sixteenth century.

PLATE 16

Medieval Industry

The Cobbler
From Dürer's The Priest of Kalenberg

33

THE GREAT SCHISM (1378-1417)

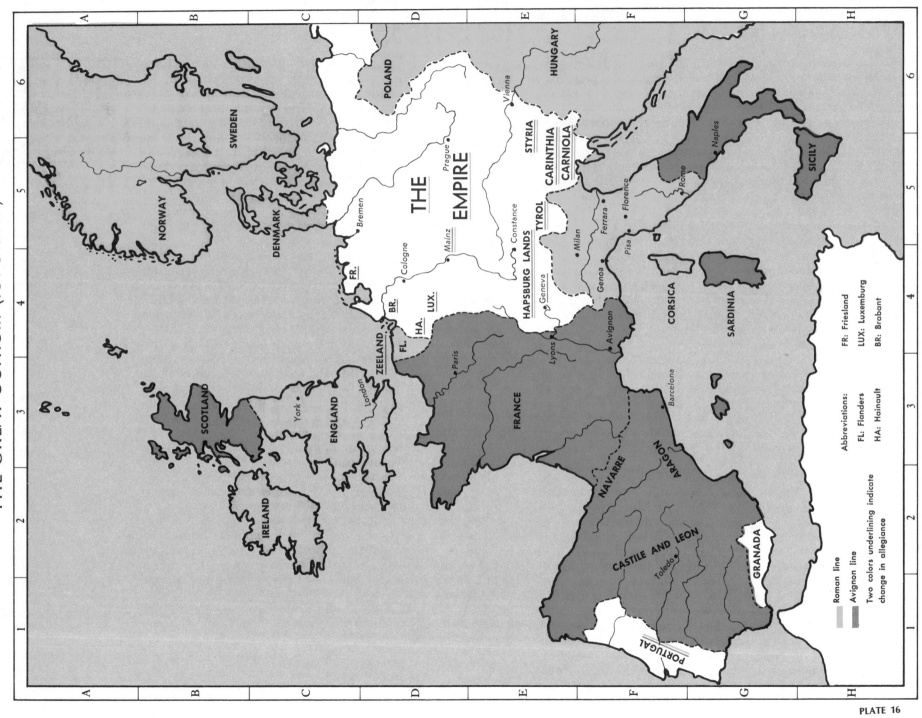

NORWAY

SWEDEN

DENMARK

POLAND

THE
EMPIRE

Prague

HUNGARY

Vienna

STYRIA

CARINTHIA

CARNIOLA

Bremen

TYROL

Constance

HAPSBURG LANDS

Cologne

Mainz

Geneva

Milan

Ferrara

Florence

Rome

Naples

SICILY

Genoa

Pisa

FR.

BR.

HA.

LUX.

FL.

ZEELAND

SCOTLAND

York

London

ENGLAND

IRELAND

Paris

FRANCE

Lyons

Avignon

Barcelona

NAVARRE

ARAGON

CORSICA

SARDINIA

CASTILE AND LEON

Toledo

GRANADA

PORTUGAL

Abbreviations:

FR: Friesland   LUX: Luxemburg

FL: Flanders   BR: Brabant

HA: Hainault

Roman line

Avignon line

Two colors underlining indicate
change in allegiance

PLATE 16

RENAISSANCE ITALY

Italy in the late fifteenth and early sixteenth centuries was divided into a multitude of minor states, none of which was able to dominate and so control and unify the peninsula. This was a land at war with itself. Weak in its several parts, Italy was a prey to outside forces. It was in this era that France began casting her eyes to the south, and several waves of invaders poured through the passes and swept down the peninsula. Charles VIII, Louis XII, and finally Francis I all tried their luck in the arena of Italy. Even imperial troops came south to attack Rome itself in 1527.

Both the empire and the papacy were weak at this time. The popes, in fact, spent much of the early Renaissance period in Avignon rather than in Rome (1309-77). The power vacuum thus created gave a great deal of freedom to the separate states and contributed to the development of the Renaissance as the cities found themselves competing for the services and attendant prestige of major artists.

One must also note the great increase of trade in this period. Even in the worst and most confused of earlier times there had always been trade in Italy—sometimes only a trickle, but still it survived. Another factor contributed to the development of the business world—finance. Great institutions, whether ecclesiastical or royal, need great amounts of money at times, and the financial houses of Italy helped provide them. A ready, urbanized labor pool, finance, production, and a successful carrying trade are important features in the Renaissance picture. The funds necessary for the sponsorship of artists and the beautification of cities came from the coffers of the trade leaders such as the Medici family in Florence.

The Florence of the Medici family was the early center of Renaissance activity. It also witnessed the great reaction to such leanings in the person and preaching of Savonarola (d. 1498). Rome next rose to prominence as haven and sponsor of art and letters. During the decline of the movement, Venice, with its commercial ideal where even art served the city, was the location of the major work. (The location of some of the most important figures of the era can be seen on plate 20.)

This was the Italy, not only of the resurgence in interest in classical studies and the concern for what it meant to be a man, but also of the power politics and maneuvering that would contribute directly to the coming of the Reformation of the sixteenth century.

PLATE 17

ROME IN THE MIDDLE AGES AND THE RENAISSANCE

Through much of the Middle Ages the city of Rome was only a shadow of its former self. The glories of the ancient days had passed, and much of the city now lay in ruins. Less than half of the area within the wall of Aurelian was inhabited around 800.

Many factors contributed to the decline evident by the Middle Ages. Barbarian invaders had come and sacked the city on more than one occasion. Sickness of epidemic proportions, including the plague, decimated the population, and those that did remain were afflicted by irregular flooding of the Tiber and a climate that was not at all healthful. The government of the city was often in the hands of bitterly feuding noble families, and even the papacy was a prize in this type of conflict. When the popes left the city in favor of Avignon there was a further decline as the papal court, monies, and artists also went to France.

For all of this the city remained the center of the Western church. The ancient division of the city into seven districts in which the main church was a "title" or cardinal church, governed by a cardinal priest, continued. The charity wards, presided over by cardinal deacons, still existed, with the addition of suburban churches led by cardinal bishops. Papal elections had been placed in the hands of these cardinals in 1059. Rome became a great center of churches, and the treasures of the whole church seemed to be concentrated there. The pilgrimage trek to the ancient basilica churches (The Seven Greater Churches of our plate) continued to draw thousands of pious believers. The march began with S.Paolo fuori le Mura, moved to S.Sebastiano, and continued until its climax at St. Peter's. The pious flocked to the city, awed by her relics and churches, and apparently not overly disturbed by the character of some of her leaders or the disrepair of the city itself.

In 1377, with the return of the papacy from Avignon, the glories of the city were gradually reborn. The ruined ancient city contributed not only land but also building materials as scavengers hauled away tons of quarried stone for the new construction. The greatest example of the new Rome was St. Peter's. The cornerstone for the new structure was laid in 1506 by Julius II, and successive popes and architects poured money and dreams into it. Bramante, Sangallo, Raphael, and Michelangelo all contributed to its design. An indulgence sale to help pay for the construction triggered the Reformation in Germany.

PLATE 18

Petrarch—a Forerunner

From a likeness, drawn by a friend, which appears in the manuscript of his last work

RENAISSANCE ITALY, around 1490

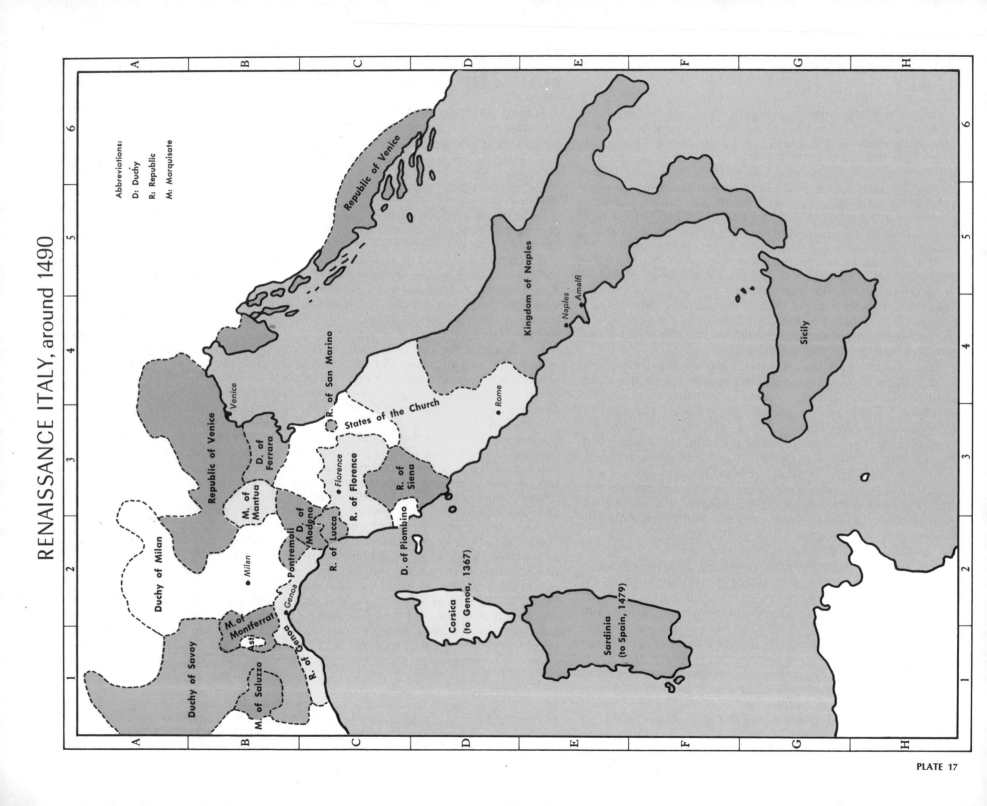

Abbreviations:
D: Duchy
R: Republic
M: Marquisate

Republic of Venice

Duchy of Milan

Venice

D. of Ferrara

M. of Mantua

D. of Modena

R. of Lucca

Pontremoli

Genoa

R. of Genoa

M. of Montferrat

Asti

Duchy of Savoy

M. of Saluzzo

Milan

R. of San Marino

States of the Church

Florence

R. of Florence

R. of Siena

D. of Piombino

Rome

Kingdom of Naples

Naples

Amalfi

Corsica
(to Genoa, 1367)

Sardinia
(to Spain, 1479)

Sicily

PLATE 17

S. Lorenzo
fuori le Mura

Via Tiburtina

Via Praenestina

Via Labicana

S. Croce
in Gerusalemme

St. John Lateran

S. Maria Maggiore

Via Latina

Via Appia

S. Sebastiano

Via Nomentana

Via Salaria

Aurelian's wall (270-75)

S. Paolo fuori le Mura

Via Ostiensis

Via Flaminia

Tiber River

Wall of
Urban VIII (1623-44)

St. Peter's

Wall of
Pope Leo IV (847-55)

Seven Greater Churches

Titular Churches of Cardinal Priests

Titular Churches of Cardinal Deacons

37

PLATE 18

THE EUROPE OF CHARLES V (c. 1519)

Charles V at 47

From a painting by Titian

Few periods in European history can equal the covey of powerful rulers that matched arms and wits during the sixteenth century. The tide of national spirit was running at its peak, and capable rulers were quick to capitalize on its potential.

In England Henry VIII (d. 1547) maneuvered and fought both the church and other encroachers. His actions and abilities are most certainly not adequately explained by reference to his succession of wives. France had Francis I (d. 1547), jealous of his own rights and also of the lands and titles of others. Far to the east and south, the Ottoman Turks under the hand of Suleiman the Magnificent (d. 1566) were beginning to cast covetous eyes toward the Christian north. Their great armies moved north to Semlin and Belgrade in 1521 and after defeating the Hungarian army at Mohacs in 1526 the heartland of Europe seemed open to them. The walls of Vienna and Güns saw the horde in 1529 and 1532 respectively.

Set in the midst of this shifting scene, Charles V. (d. 1558), the emperor, tried to maintain order, repel the advances of the Turks, heal the schism of the church, and defend and increase his own hereditary holdings. His base of power was Spain which was his as a descendant of Ferdinand and Isabella. The last of the Moslems had been driven from the peninsula in 1492 when Granada had fallen. The generations of struggle had helped create a strong national church and had also helped make the Spanish military machine one of the most effective in Europe. Charles also received Sardinia, Sicily, Naples, and the Balearic Islands from Ferdinand and Isabella. In addition to this the Spanish territories in North, Central, and South America poured the riches of the New World into his treasury.

From his paternal grandmother, Mary of Burgundy, he inherited the larger part of the Netherlands, Franche Comte, and Luxemburg, while from Maximilian, his paternal grandfather, the Hapsburg lands of Germany fell to him. A few years later the eastern flank of the Empire (Hungary, Bohemia, Moravia, and Silesia) was also claimed by the Hapsburg dynasty.

Perhaps a simple diagram would clarify the dynastic picture:

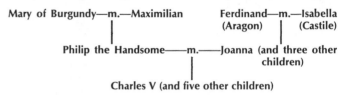

In 1519 he was elected emperor and so became, in name at least, the sovereign of the central lands of Europe also. Charles's holdings and dynastic ambitions did not allow him an easy rule.

The territorial aspirations of Charles and Francis I brought them into conflict. Both claimed the Kingdom of Naples, Milan, Burgundy, and Flanders and Artois. A whole series of Hapsburg-Valois wars disturbed Europe due to these conflicting claims and ambitions.

There was also a pointed rivalry between the Pope and Charles. The popes as secular rulers were deeply involved in the power politics of the day. The church, with its vast holdings of land, was a powerful force. It was a part of papal policy that the same force should not be allowed to control both Naples and Milan. The Pope, therefore, often cast his lot with Francis in opposition to Charles. Leo X favored Francis over Charles in the imperial elections, and Clement VII actually allied himself with the French king at the very time when concerted action with Charles could have crushed the Reformation. This type of maneuvering would itself aid the Reformation as would the incursions of the Turks.

Leo X

From a painting by Raphael

Francis I

From a painting by Clouet

38

PLATE 19

THE EUROPE OF CHARLES V (c.1519)

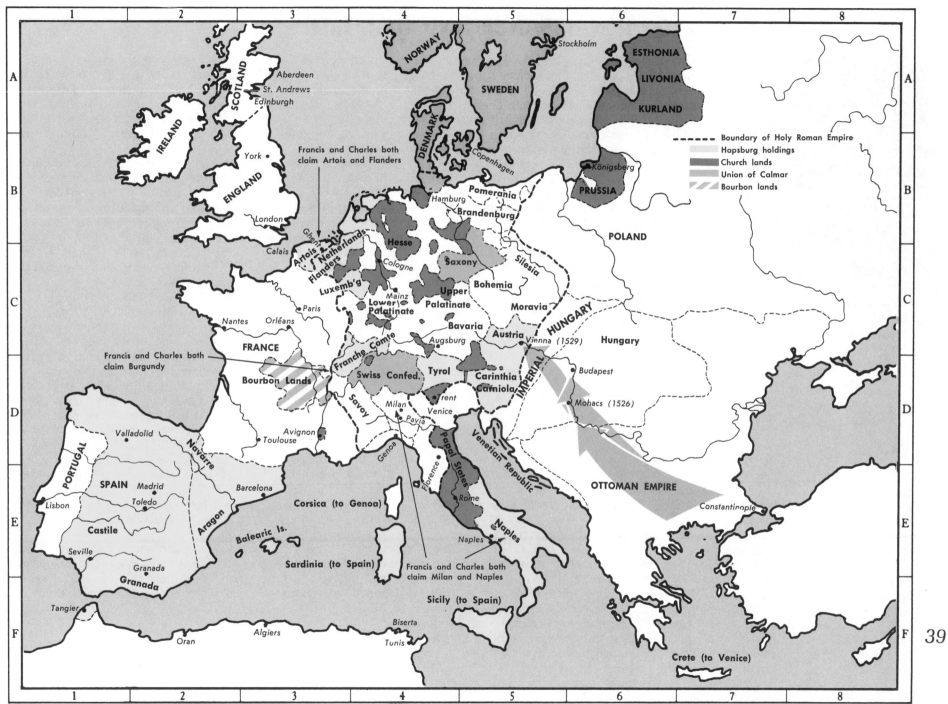

Boundary of Holy Roman Empire
Hapsburg holdings
Church lands
Union of Calmar
Bourbon lands

NORWAY
SWEDEN
Stockholm
ESTHONIA
LIVONIA
KURLAND
IRELAND
SCOTLAND
Aberdeen
St. Andrews
Edinburgh
York
ENGLAND
London
Calais
Königsberg
PRUSSIA
POLAND
Francis and Charles both claim Artois and Flanders
Hamburg
Pomerania
Brandenburg
Ghent
Artois
Netherlands
Flanders
Hesse
Cologne
Saxony
Silesia
Luxemb'g
Mainz
Upper
Palatinate
Bohemia
Lower
Palatinate
Moravia
Nantes
Orléans
Paris
Bavaria
HUNGARY
FRANCE
Augsburg
Austria
Vienna (1529)
Hungary
Francis and Charles both claim Burgundy
Franche Comté
Swiss Confed.
Tyrol
Carinthia
Carniola
IMPERIAL
Budapest
Bourbon Lands
Savoy
Trent
Milan
Venice
Mohacs (1526)
Pavia
Genoa
Avignon
Toulouse
Valladolid
Navarre
PORTUGAL
SPAIN
Madrid
Barcelona
Aragon
Corsica (to Genoa)
Papal States
Venetian Republic
OTTOMAN EMPIRE
Florence
Lisbon
Castile
Toledo
Rome
Constantinople
Seville
Balearic Is.
Naples
Granada
Sardinia (to Spain)
Naples
Francis and Charles both claim Milan and Naples
Granada
Sicily (to Spain)
Tangier
Biserta
Algiers
Crete (to Venice)
Oran
Tunis
DENMARK
Copenhagen

39

PLATE 19

THE AGE OF RENAISSANCE AND DISCOVERY

Erasmus—The Prince of the Humanists

From a painting by Hans Holbein the Younger

It was an exciting age when man rediscovered himself and his world. Under the tutelage of the ancients, mediated by men like Petrarch, Dante, and Marsilius of Ficino, the person of the late fourteenth, fifteenth, and sixteenth centuries found new concern for, and understanding of, what it meant to be a man. Repelled by the venality and barbarism of his own day, Petrarch (d. 1374) had retired from the papal court at Avignon to the more peaceful world of nature and the more orderly realm of the ancients. Both of these emphases would be magnified hundreds of times by his successors. In the plastic arts of the Renaissance the power of nature is overwhelming while its literature springs from the seed bed of classical Greece and Rome.

In Florence, for example, the council called a Byzantine scholar, Manuel Chrysoloras, to teach Greek and philosophy. By 1429 the city was no longer dependent upon Greeks to teach the language, and in the meantime other cities had begun importing instructors. The study of classical Hellenism went beyond linguistics. Platonic studies rose to colossal proportions, and a Platonic Academy was founded in Florence in the 1470's.

The concern for ancient texts and languages had great effect on biblical studies. *Ad Fontes,* "To the sources," was the cry as men like Ximenes, Reuchlin, and Erasmus led the way to the Hebrew and Greek texts of the Bible. The texts, commentaries, and other writings that poured from Humanistic pens were quickly disseminated via the printing press, itself a wonder of the age. The Humanists of the north were also concerned with reform in the church. Their efforts created an atmosphere conducive to the Reformation in some areas. Some Humanists themselves later became identified with the Reformation forces.

This was an age of *re*covery of the past and also *dis*covery of man and the world. The Renaissance man came to see himself as an individual—a person of power. What counted was not birth and nobility, but one's wit and drive. The ideal was the perfection of the individual in the many-sided man. All this was in sharp contrast to the basic collectivism and static system of the Middle Ages. The boundaries imposed in many instances by medieval culture and the church were eroding as the glories and capabilities of the human person again became of paramount concern. The emphasis could be, and was, both Christian and pagan. In the north, as we have noted, the Human-

ists concerned themselves with purifying the church and personal life, with developing *humanitas* by a return to the purity of the ancients and the early church. Erasmus of Rotterdam (d. 1536) exemplifies this northern movement. In the south there was often a reveling in not only the virtues but also the vices of antiquity. The result was not always helpful to the church.

The discovery of nature is seen best in art. The difference between the anonymous painters of symbolic figures of the Middle Ages and the self-aware realists of the Renaissance, glorying in the beauties of nature and mankind, is a tremendous one. The art of painting and sculpture leaped forward, supported by the wealth of individual patrons, cities, or popes. Whatever Renaissance popes such as Julius II, Leo X, and Clement VII were not, they should be remembered positively for their patronage of the art of their day.

Man not only discovered himself in this era, but also his world. Concern for natural science multiplied. Medicine began recovering from its superstitious illness of the Middle Ages as the study of anatomy revealed some of the secrets of the body, the use of quarantine restricted contagious diseases, and hospitals multiplied. The stars and their courses occupied others, although astrology still occupied the center stage, and even the educated believed that the stars somehow determined events on earth. Mathematicians like Pacioli wrote widely, desiring to place their theoretical knowledge into the hands of the world. Led by men like Toscanelli, Paciolo, and Leonardo da Vinci, Italy held the highest place in the European world for mathematics and natural science in the late fifteenth century. The learned of other lands, e.g. Regiomontanus and Copernicus, acknowledged that they were pupils of the Italians.

Commercial concern plus an indomitable curiosity prodded Columbus, Magellan, Cabot, Cartier, Hudson, and others to venture out on the unknown seas, and another new world was opened. Our plate attempts to place some of the more prominent figures of the era and the centers of their work. Representative voyages are also indicated, at least as to point of origin.

40

PLATE 20

THE AGE OF RENAISSANCE AND DISCOVERY

Danzig
Königsberg
Thorn
Regiomontanus, 1436
Lübeck
Bremen
Agricola, 1443
Wittenberg
Luther, 1483
Van Eyck, 1381
Cologne
Louvain Massys, 1460
Erfurt
Behaim, 1430
Prague
Van de Wyden, 1400
Hutten, 1488
Mainz
Dürer, 1471
Nürnberg
Gutenberg, 1397
Melanchthon, 1497
Reuchlin, 1455
Regensburg (Ratisbon)
Augsburg
Vienna
Holbein, 1497
Buda
Constance
Zwingli, 1484
Basel
Zürich
Paracelsus, 1493
Geneva
Titian, 1477
Giorgione, 1478
Trent
Bellini, 1400
Alberti, 1404
Michelangelo
Petrarch, 1303
L. Bruni, 1492
Aretino, 1441
Savonarola, 1452
Perugia
S. Aeneas Sylvius
Rome
Florence
Pisa Siena
Signorelli,
Ferrara
Venice
Milan
Bologna
da Vinci, 1452
Aeneas Sylvius 1405
L. Valla, 1405
Lucrezia Borgia (1480)
Genoa
Brunelleschi, 1377
Donatello, 1386
Fra Filippo Lippi, 1406
Ficino, 1433
Botticelli, 1447
Lorenzo Medici, 1449
Americus Vespucius, 1451
Machiavelli, 1469
Guicciardini, 1483
del Sarto, 1486
B. Cellini, 1500
Avignon
Cabot, 1450
Columbus, 1451
Marseilles
Leiden
Rotterdam
Erasmus
Bruges
Bruges
Comines, 1445
Chartier, 1392
Gossart, 1470
Noyon
Calvin, 1509
Trier
Boccaccio, 1313
Chas. of Orleans, 1391
Villon, 1430
Paris
Dijon
Moulins
Bruegel 1520
Colet, 1466
More, 1478
Canterbury
Linacre, 1480
LeFevre, 1455
Paré, 1510
Fontainebleau
Blois
Chambord
Amboise
Rabelais, 1490
Angoulême
Marguerite of Navarre, 1492
Bordeaux
Azay-le-Rideau
Tours
John Knox 1505
Edinburgh
Coverdale 1488
Cranmer, 1489
Oxford
Wyatt, 1503
London
Caxton, 1422
St. Malo

Covilha, 1487 (to India)

Servetus, 1511
Ximenes, 1438
Madrid
Loyola, 1480
Magellan, 1480
Barcelona
Lisbon
Vasco Da Gama, 1450
San Lucar
Palos
Seville
Las Casas, 1474

Voyages

Hudson, 1609
Chancellor, 1553
Barents, 1596, 1609
Hudson, 1610
Davis, 1587
Davis, 1585
Davis, 1586
Sebastian Cabot, 1508
John Cabot, 1497
Frobischer, 1576-8
Baffin, 1616
Cartier, 1534-5
Cartier, 1535-6
Verrazano, 1524
Corte Real, 1500, 1501
Cao, 1482
da Gama, 1497
Cabral, 1500
Columbus, 1492-93;
Columbus, 1497
Vespucci, 1502
Magellan, 1519
Vespucci, 1499

VOYAGES: Spanish -----   Dutch -----   English -----   French -----   Portuguese -----
Red: Representative Renaissance-Humanist Figures

41

PLATE 20

THE LUTHER LANDS

Martin Luther, c. 1525

From a painting by Lucas Cranach the Elder

In the sixteenth century the frontier town of Wittenberg provided the center for a movement that would shake the foundations of structures once considered eternal. Both Empire and Papacy would be challenged by the concern and fire of a monk from the university in this small town.

The "Luther Lands," properly speaking, are bounded by the Erzgebirge (Bohemian Massif) on the southeast, Electoral Saxony a bit above Wittenberg in the northeast, the Harz Mountains in the northwest, and the Thuringian Forest area around the Wartburg in the southwest. The relative smallness of this arena of action is seen when one notes that no city within it is more than around seventy-five miles from Wittenberg.

Luther's early years were spent in the rolling foothills of the Harz Mountains. When he moved south to Erfurt he found a more level area, and his final trek to Wittenberg took him to the Elbe River valley which is very nearly flat. The basin between the mountains is drained by the Mulde, the Saale, and the Elbe. These rivers figure in Luther's correspondence, as does the beauty of the mountains around the Wartburg.

Luther himself was not widely traveled, even for his day. His efforts were largely limited to Electoral Saxony. Since 1483 Saxony had been divided into two parts, Ernestine and Albertine, or Electoral and Ducal, respectively. It was Luther's good fortune to live in Electoral Saxony during his career as a reformer. His ruler, the Elector Frederick the Wise, protected him when both empire and church had turned against him. Ducal Saxony, on the other hand, was ruled by Duke George, a staunch Catholic and opponent of Luther. The famous Leipzig debate took place in his territory.

Ducal Saxony became Protestant at the death of George, but the ancient rivalry between the two parts continued. Maurice of Saxony (ducal) allied himself with Charles V and attacked Electoral Saxony during the Schmalcaldic War (1546-7). In return he received the Electoral post and part of the Ernestine lands.

Luther was born in Eisleben, a small mining town in northeast Germany, grew up in Mansfeld, and was educated in Eisenach, Magdeburg, and Erfurt. Shortly after receiving his M.A. at the university he became a monk, a member of the Augustinians in Erfurt. Later ordained, he studied theology and rose through the academic ranks at Erfurt. Transferred to the new University of Wittenberg in 1511, he was associated with that school for the remainder of his life. His role as a Doctor of Theology and as a teacher of successive generations of university students is often forgotten when one emphasizes only his efforts at reforming the church.

Before being declared an outlaw by the Emperor, Luther had traveled to Rome (1510) and Cologne (1512) on monastic business, to Heidelberg (1518) to defend a set of theses in debate before his Augustinian order, and to Augsburg (1518) to speak to Cardinal Cajetan about alleged errors in the matter of indulgences. In 1520 he ventured to the west to Worms where a dramatic confrontation with the Emperor occurred. The year 1529 took him west to Marburg for a discussion with Zwingli and others of the Swiss and south German Reformation parties.

The limits of Luther's travels in Germany, then, were Augsburg in the south and Worms, Cologne, and Marburg in the west. Most of his days were spent within the narrower limits of Saxony. A wider area is included on this plate however, to show some of the other important places of the Reformer's day. The legend on the plate itself refers to several specific locations associated with his career.

Frederick the Wise, Elector of Saxony

Luther's Protector
By Albrecht Dürer, c. 1524

Duke George of Saxony

Ruler of Ducal Saxony
Lucas Cranach the Elder

PLATE 21

42

THE LUTHER LANDS

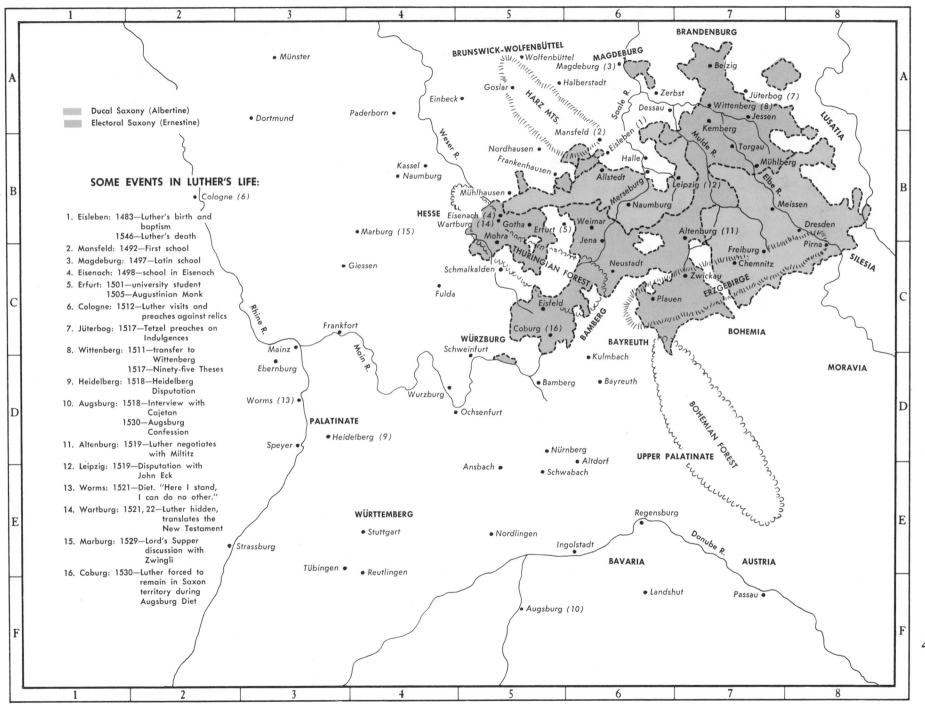

Ducal Saxony (Albertine)
Electoral Saxony (Ernestine)

SOME EVENTS IN LUTHER'S LIFE:

1. Eisleben: 1483—Luther's birth and
   baptism
   1546—Luther's death
2. Mansfeld: 1492—First school
3. Magdeburg: 1497—Latin school
4. Eisenach: 1498—school in Eisenach
5. Erfurt: 1501—university student
   1505—Augustinian Monk
6. Cologne: 1512—Luther visits and
   preaches against relics
7. Jüterbog: 1517—Tetzel preaches on
   Indulgences
8. Wittenberg: 1511—transfer to
   Wittenberg
   1517—Ninety-five Theses
9. Heidelberg: 1518—Heidelberg
   Disputation
10. Augsburg: 1518—Interview with
    Cajetan
    1530—Augsburg
    Confession
11. Altenburg: 1519—Luther negotiates
    with Miltitz
12. Leipzig: 1519—Disputation with
    John Eck
13. Worms: 1521—Diet. "Here I stand,
    I can do no other."
14. Wartburg: 1521, 22—Luther hidden,
    translates the
    New Testament
15. Marburg: 1529—Lord's Supper
    discussion with
    Zwingli
16. Coburg: 1530—Luther forced to
    remain in Saxon
    territory during
    Augsburg Diet

Map labels

BRANDENBURG
BRUNSWICK-WOLFENBÜTTEL
MAGDEBURG
• Münster
• Wolfenbüttel
Magdeburg (3)
• Belzig
• Halberstadt
Goslar •
• Zerbst
• Jüterbog (7)
Einbeck •
Wittenberg (8)
HARZ MTS.
Dessau •
• Jessen
LUSATIA
• Dortmund
Paderborn •
Saale R.
Mansfeld (2)
Kemberg •
• Torgau
Nordhausen •
Eisleben (1)
Mulde R.
• Mühlberg
Frankenhausen •
Halle •
Elbe R.
Kassel •
Allstedt •
• Leipzig (12)
• Meissen
• Naumburg
Mühlhausen •
Merseburg •
HESSE
Eisenach (4)
• Naumburg
Dresden •
Wartburg (14) Gotha •
Weimar
Altenburg (11)
• Pirna
• Marburg (15)
Mohra •
Erfurt (5)
Freiburg •
SILESIA
Jena
Chemnitz •
• Giessen
Schmalkalden •
Neustadt
THURINGIAN FOREST
• Zwickau
ERZGEBIRGE
• Fulda
Eisfeld •
Plauen •
BOHEMIA
Coburg (16)
BAMBERG
BAYREUTH
Rhine R.
MORAVIA
• Frankfurt
WÜRZBURG
Schweinfurt •
• Kulmbach
Mainz •
• Bamberg
• Bayreuth
BOHEMIAN FOREST
Ebernburg •
Wurzburg •
Main R.
PALATINATE
Worms (13) •
• Ochsenfurt
UPPER PALATINATE
Speyer •
Heidelberg (9) •
• Nürnberg
• Altdorf
Ansbach •
• Schwabach
Regensburg •
WÜRTTEMBERG
• Nordlingen
Danube R.
AUSTRIA
Strassburg •
• Stuttgart
Ingolstadt •
Tübingen •
• Reutlingen
BAVARIA
• Landshut
Passau •
• Augsburg (10)

43

PLATE 21

EXPANSION OF THE REFORMATION. The Religious Situation Around 1529

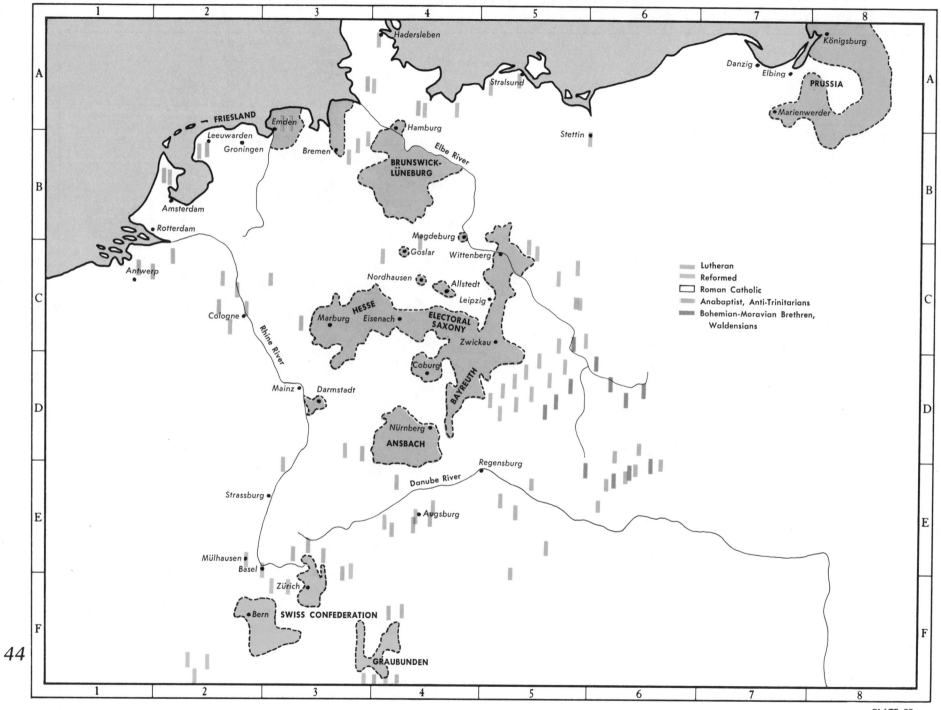

Legend:
- Lutheran
- Reformed
- Roman Catholic
- Anabaptist, Anti-Trinitarians
- Bohemian-Moravian Brethren, Waldensians

Map labels: Hadersleben, Königsburg, Danzig, Elbing, PRUSSIA, Marienwerder, Stralsund, FRIESLAND, Emden, Leeuwarden, Groningen, Bremen, Hamburg, Elbe River, Stettin, BRUNSWICK-LÜNEBURG, Amsterdam, Rotterdam, Magdeburg, Goslar, Wittenberg, Antwerp, Nordhausen, Allstedt, Leipzig, Cologne, HESSE, Marburg, Eisenach, ELECTORAL SAXONY, Zwickau, Rhine River, Coburg, Mainz, Darmstadt, BAYREUTH, Nürnberg, ANSBACH, Regensburg, Strassburg, Danube River, Augsburg, Mülhausen, Basel, Zürich, Bern, SWISS CONFEDERATION, GRAUBUNDEN

44

PLATE 22

ONE HUNDRED YEARS OF SHIFTING BOUNDARIES: 1529, 1555, 1618

In 1529, the year before the Diet at Augsburg at which the Statement of Faith of the Protestants was presented, the land controlled by these forces was still rather limited. The heart areas of Saxony, Hesse, Brunswick-Lüneberg, and Ansbach were surrounded by strongly Catholic lands. Minor outposts were scattered about, but they too were isolated. The same situation prevailed in the south where the Reformed strength was centered.

The Lutheran forces had survived several potentially disastrous events in the mid-1520's. The problems with the Enthusiasts had led to open conflict and some defections, as had the written debate between Luther and Erasmus regarding the Freedom of the Will. Of equal importance was the Peasant Revolt and the resultant loss to the Lutherans of much of their lower-class support.

In spite of these reverses the movement had expanded since Charles, having promulgated the Edict of Worms that made Luther an outlaw (1521), had left the country, not to return until 1530. In his absence Germany was supposed to be ruled by an Imperial Supreme Court, a Regency Council, and legislative assemblies (Diets). There were several Diets that took no real action against the Lutherans. The Diet of Speyer in 1526 had issued an ambiguous statement that "Every estate should so live, rule and believe as he may hope to answer to God and his imperial majesty." The goal of this sentence was not clear; the Lutherans however used it to justify their actions, and in Saxony and Hesse the Lutheran Church was established. The Diet of Speyer of 1529 tried, through its Catholic majority, to forbid the spread of Lutheranism and to insure toleration for Catholics in Lutheran territories. The Lutheran princes "protested" this action (thus originating the term Protestants) and the emperor was prevailed upon by his counselors to give them an opportunity to explain their faith. This led to the Diet of Augsburg and the Augsburg Confession (1530).

The long absence of Charles V from Germany was caused by revolt in Spain in the early 1520's, and the pressures of Francis I and Suleiman. The nine-year period of imperial inaction in Germany was of immeasurable benefit to the Reformation.

The second plate (23) indicates how the situation had changed by the signing of the Peace of Augsburg in 1555. In 1546 Charles had finally had opportunity to move against the Lutherans. That this had always been his intent was clear as far back as the Diet of Worms in 1521, but he had been hampered by almost continual conflict with Francis I and Suleiman. Even the popes had hindered him, not intentionally of course. Twenty-five years had elapsed, but now he could act. The ensuing Schmalcaldic War, a story complete with almost comic errors by the Lutherans, treachery by Maurice of Saxony, and tactical shrewdness by the emperor, had led to an attempt to settle the religious issues without a church council. This attempt, a compromise called an Interim, was unacceptable to Protestants and Catholics. Only the presence of Spanish occupation troops in northern Europe kept the Interim in effect. Revolt, or the so-called War of Liberation, followed in which Maurice changed sides again, Henry II of France assisted against his family foe, the emperor, and Charles himself, enjoying peace and almost universal victory one day, was forced to flee for safety through the snow-swept Alps on the next. The Peace of Augsburg (1555) showed no real loss of land by the Lutherans, but rather a significant gain when compared to the situation in 1529.

By 1618, the year in which the Thirty Years' War broke out, the religious map of central Europe had become more complex. One notes the expansion of the Reformed groups, especially those who looked to Calvin. Large areas have been lost by the Lutherans to the aggressive Calvinists, including the Palatinate, Ansbach, and Hesse. Other places, notably Brandenburg, now were mixed Lutheran and Calvinist instead of being all Lutheran as earlier. Strong bodies of Calvinists existed in Hungary. The Magyars had preferred Calvinism to the early Lutheranism which was associated with German domination of Hungary.

One also notes the power of the Counter-Reformation in reclaiming lands lost earlier. Some territories, of course, had remained loyal to Rome, but the concentrated efforts of the Jesuits in particular had succeeded in bringing others back to the fold.

The largest Reformation group continued to be the Lutheran. Having weathered the storms of the Schmalcaldic War, the Interims, and the War of Liberation, this body was now stabilized behind its northern bastions. The divisions thus marked would continue, unchanged in the main, into the modern era.

PLATES 22, 23, and 24

Maurice of Saxony
Lucas Cranach the Younger, c. 1553

45

EXPANSION OF THE REFORMATION. Situation Around 1555

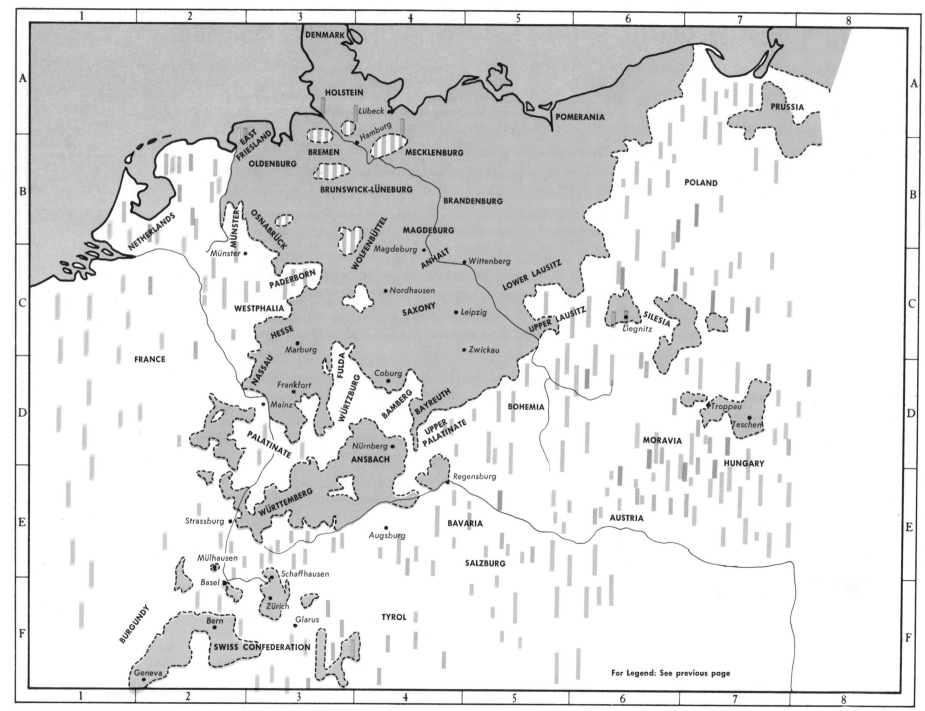

DENMARK

HOLSTEIN
Lübeck
Hamburg
EAST FRIESLAND
BREMEN
OLDENBURG
MECKLENBURG
POMERANIA
PRUSSIA
POLAND
NETHERLANDS
MÜNSTER
OSNABRÜCK
BRUNSWICK-LÜNEBURG
BRANDENBURG
Münster
WOLFENBÜTTEL
MAGDEBURG
Magdeburg
ANHALT
Wittenberg
PADERBORN
LOWER LAUSITZ
Nordhausen
WESTPHALIA
SAXONY
Leipzig
UPPER LAUSITZ
SILESIA
Liegnitz
HESSE
Marburg
Zwickau
FRANCE
NASSAU
FULDA
Coburg
WÜRZBURG
BAMBERG
BAYREUTH
BOHEMIA
MORAVIA
Troppau
Frankfort
Teschen
Mainz
PALATINATE
UPPER PALATINATE
HUNGARY
Nürnberg
ANSBACH
Regensburg
WÜRTTEMBERG
AUSTRIA
Strassburg
BAVARIA
Augsburg
Mülhausen
SALZBURG
Basel
Schaffhausen
Zürich
Glarus
TYROL
BURGUNDY
Bern
SWISS CONFEDERATION
Geneva

For Legend: See previous page

46

PLATE 23

EUROPEAN RELIGIOUS SITUATION AROUND 1618

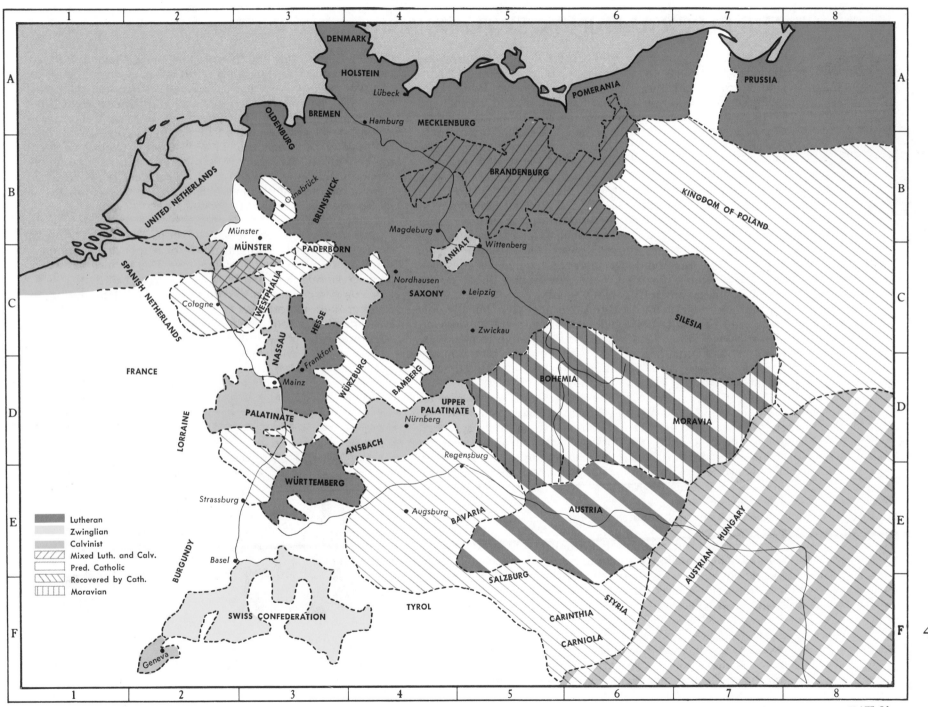

Legend:

- Lutheran
- Zwinglian
- Calvinist
- Mixed Luth. and Calv.
- Pred. Catholic
- Recovered by Cath.
- Moravian

DENMARK
HOLSTEIN
Lübeck
BREMEN
OLDENBURG
Hamburg
MECKLENBURG
POMERANIA
PRUSSIA

UNITED NETHERLANDS
Osnabrück
BRUNSWICK
BRANDENBURG
KINGDOM OF POLAND

Münster
MÜNSTER
PADERBORN
Magdeburg
ANHALT
Wittenberg

SPANISH NETHERLANDS
Cologne
WESTPHALIA
Nordhausen
SAXONY
Leipzig
SILESIA

HESSE
Zwickau

NASSAU
Frankfort
WÜRZBURG
BAMBERG
BOHEMIA

FRANCE
Mainz
UPPER
PALATINATE
MORAVIA

LORRAINE
PALATINATE
ANSBACH
Nürnberg

Regensburg
WÜRTTEMBERG
AUSTRIA
AUSTRIAN HUNGARY

Strassburg
Augsburg
BAVARIA

BURGUNDY
Basel
SALZBURG
STYRIA

SWISS CONFEDERATION
TYROL
CARINTHIA

Geneva
CARNIOLA

47

PLATE 24

THE REFORMATION IN SWITZERLAND

Ulrich Zwingli
By Hans Asper

Ulrich Zwingli, preacher in Zurich following 1519, provided the needed impulse to reform in German-speaking Switzerland. Born in 1484 in Wildhaus in northeast Switzerland, Zwingli had a good education at Basel, Bern, and Vienna, and in 1506, having received his M.A., was ordained a priest at Glarus. After serving in Glarus and Einsiedeln, he came to Zurich. He moved through Erasmian humanism under the influence of the Fathers and Luther to the stance of a reformer. His position became the official one in the canton through a series of three debates before the city council in 1523 and 1524. Bern accepted the new ways as Zwingli played on its pride as an independent canton and thus thwarted the wishes of a territorial Diet. Basel, led by Johann Oecolampadius, Saint Gall, and other centers moved toward the Zwinglian camp.

In 1524 the four mountain cantons, traditionally conservative, formed the Christian Union to resist the threat of the heresy of the commercial cantons such as Zurich. The Zwinglians formed their own Christian Alliance in 1527. Initially only Zurich and Constance belonged, later many others joined. German-speaking Switzerland was thus divided over religious issues, just as Germany itself had split into two camps in the Catholic Alliance of Regensburg (1524) and the Lutheran League of Torgau (1526).

Zwingli, both spiritual reformer and politician, was eager for agreements to further the Protestant cause. Although several years of debate with Luther on the Lord's Supper had embittered both sides, the goal of a political union with the Germans led the Zurichers to march north to Marburg, a castle of Philip of Hesse, for a discussion with the Lutherans in 1529. (See plate 21.) This trip marked Zwingli's farthest venture to the north.

Later in 1529 he turned to force in order to establish evangelical preaching in the mountain cantons. He attempted to cut off food, and particularly salt, from the conservatives. The hope was that this blockade would force them to yield. War was at hand, but was averted, only to break out in 1531 when a new blockade caused the Second Cappel War, in which Zwingli was killed.

The towering figure in French-speaking Switzerland was John Calvin (d. 1564). Born in France in 1509 and educated as a lawyer and humanist, Calvin arrived in Geneva in 1536, already a famous young man because of his great work, *The Institutes of the Christian Religion*. He was prevailed upon by William Farel to stay and labor in that city. Geneva had already experienced a type of political reformation in which the Bishop of Savoy had been ousted, and Farel had labored with small success to give some spiritual reality to the change. When Calvin arrived, bound for Strassburg to devote himself to writing, Farel virtually forced him to stay. The two were expelled after two years, but in 1541 Calvin returned to spend the rest of his days there. His influence spread through the Genevan Academy and through the refugees who flocked to Geneva only to return home again carrying the reformation in its Genevan garb. Calvin's work has been perpetuated in the Reformed churches of the world.

After nearly ten years of negotiations the famous Consensus Tigurinus (1549) brought the German-speaking and French-speaking Reformation parties together. This alliance has weathered the storms of time.

A comparable Catholic union was established during the Counter-Reformation days in the Borromean League of 1589. Switzerland was thus divided in a religious sense. The basic lines of division have continued to this day.

John Calvin
Artist unknown

John Oecolampadius
From Beza's Icons

PLATE 25

THE REFORMATION IN SWITZERLAND

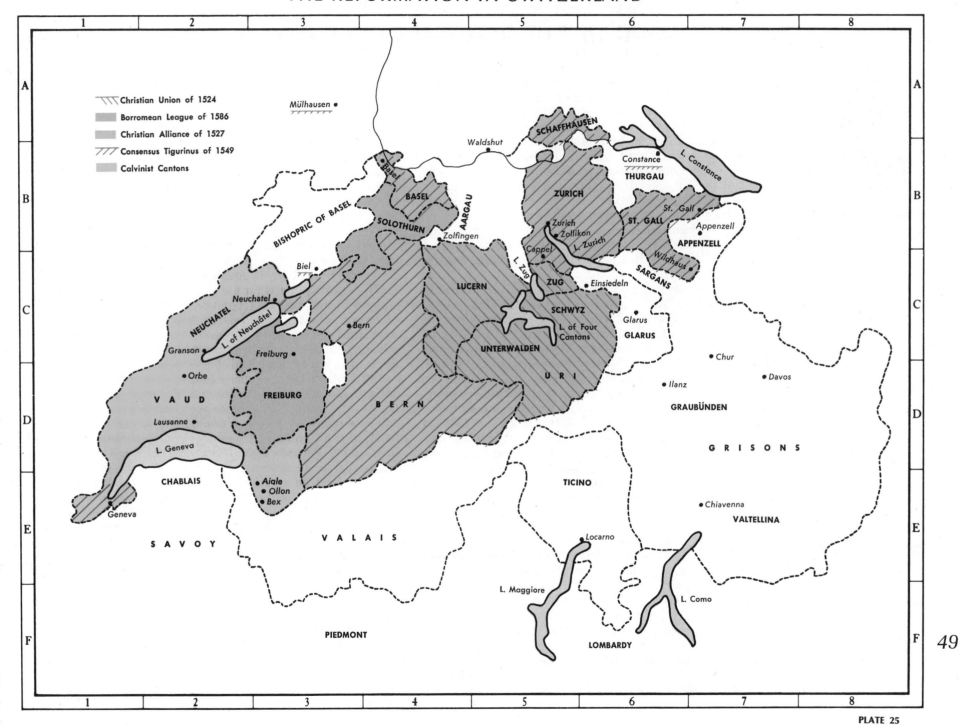

Christian Union of 1524
Borromean League of 1586
Christian Alliance of 1527
Consensus Tigurinus of 1549
Calvinist Cantons

Mülhausen

Waldshut

SCHAFFHAUSEN

Constance
L. Constance

THURGAU

ZURICH

Basel

BASEL

SOLOTHURN

AARGAU

Zofingen

BISHOPRIC OF BASEL

St. Gall

ST. GALL

Appenzell

APPENZELL

Zurich
Zollikon

Biel

Cappel

L. Zurich

Wildhaus

SARGANS

Neuchatel

NEUCHATEL

L. of Neuchâtel

Einsiedeln

LUCERN

L. Zug

ZUG

Glarus

Granson

Bern

SCHWYZ

GLARUS

Chur

Orbe

Freiburg

L. of Four
Cantons

Ilanz

Davos

VAUD

FREIBURG

UNTERWALDEN

URI

GRAUBÜNDEN

BERN

Lausanne

GRISONS

L. Geneva

CHABLAIS

Aigle
Ollon
Bex

VALAIS

Chiavenna

VALTELLINA

Geneva

SAVOY

TICINO

Locarno

PIEDMONT

L. Maggiore

L. Como

LOMBARDY

THE LEFT WING OF THE REFORMATION: Concentration and Expansion

Balthasar Hubmaier
From an old woodcut

Beginning as an offshoot of the Zwinglian Reformation in Zurich, the Anabaptists, or Brethren, spread rapidly to other areas. The assumption, made by most of the mainline reformers of the sixteenth century and perpetuated by figures like Holl and Boehmer, that the early Swiss Brethren were to be linked with the radical movement of Thomas Müntzer (d. 1525), has been demonstrated as untenable by recent Mennonite scholars. There were some letters exchanged between Müntzer and Grebel, but they disagreed on more points than they agreed upon. The militant, apocalyptic character of Müntzer was in direct contrast to the quietism and pacifism of the southern group. Certain individuals, such as Hans Hut of the south German movement, were momentarily taken by Müntzer, but experienced a change of heart after the failure of the Peasants' Revolt at Frankenhausen.

The movement spread with great speed. The fact of persistent persecution in both Roman and Protestant areas, in the one for heresy, in the other for sedition, contributed to the rapid expansion. Within four or five years of its founding all but one of its early leaders had been martyred. Conrad Grebel, the exception, died of the plague while waiting trial in prison.

Another factor in the expansion was missionary concern. To the Anabaptist the religious life was to be an active, even aggressive, discipleship. One feature of this mission outreach was mass baptisms. At Münster in 1534 there were 1,400 in a week and at times nearly whole villages would be baptized in one ceremony. The program for mission expansion was coordinated at a synod meeting (later called the "Martyrs' Synod" because of the fate of so many of its participants) in Augsburg in 1527. Whole towns were at times briefly controlled by the group: Hallau, Waldshut, Nicolsburg, and Münster.

The movement spread to south Germany, and Augsburg became an early center. Leaders such as Hans Denck and Hans Hut contributed to its development. Another area of growth was Moravia where a period of toleration was enjoyed. Balthasar Hubmaier, Jacob Hutter, and others led there.

In the Rhine Valley the city of Strassburg provided a haven of toleration, as did the lands of Philip of Hesse to the north. One of the Anabaptist leaders in Strassburg assumed a radical position, departing from the basic pacifism of the main group, and proceeded down the Rhine to the Low Countries, preaching an apocalyptic message. This man, Melchior Hoffman, planted the seeds in the north from which fruit of a very radical nature would spring. Some wished to establish the kingdom "without tarrying for any," and managed to seize control of the city of Münster. Under the leadership of Jan Matthys and John of Leyden, a theocratic kingdom was established. To outsiders it symbolized both heresy and political rebellion. After a bitter siege the city fell and the radicals were destroyed (1535). The fall of Münster marked the end, practically speaking, of the militant variety of Anabaptism. A great wave of persecution swept over Europe and thousands were killed. The Münster debacle gave new impetus to the quietistic type. This remnant, and others who had never succumbed to the use of the sword were gathered together by men like Menno Simons (d. 1559) and led in quietistic ways closely related to the earlier Swiss Brethren.

Modern Christianity is deeply indebted to this martyr church for its major emphasis on the congregational system of polity, along with the absolute separation of church and state and the notion of voluntarism in relation to church membership. The Anabaptists were also the forerunners in the whole matter of religious freedom, a concept not really shared by either Catholic or mainline Protestant in the sixteenth century.

Antitrinitarianism is initially asociated with Lelio and Fausto Socinus and with Servetus. Some of the Anabaptists, e.g. Hans Denck, had antitrinitarian tendencies, but this was never a general characteristic. Never a popular movement, it had been harassed from one area to another and had found its greatest opportunity for growth and safety in Poland. The Grisons, a relatively tolerant and isolated area, was an early refugee center for both Italy and Zurich. There were antitrinitarian groups even in Geneva after Servetus' death (1553) as Italian refugees continued to question the traditional doctrine. Forcefully put down in Geneva, Zurich, and Basel, the proponents moved to Transylvania and Poland where the Italians exerted strong influence (Biandrata, Alciati, and Gentile). Rakow, a town with religious freedom, was the scene of rapid growth. The Racovian Catechism (1605) is evidence of this vitality. Orthodox Protestant parties plus the introduction of the Jesuits in 1564 led to eventual suppression. England was another place to which Socinianism spread, especially under John Biddle (d. 1662), and it was from England that its influence reached the New World.

PLATE 26

THE LEFT WING OF THE REFORMATION: Concentration and Expansion

Map labels:

Flensburg · Danzig · DUCAL PRUSSIA · Rastenburg · ROYAL PRUSSIA · Elbing · Marienwerder · Lübeck · Wismar · FRISIA · Emden · Dokkum · Leeuwarden · Oldenburg · Witmarsum · Wegrou · Norwich · ENGLAND · Haarlem · Amsterdam · Deventer · Warsaw · Brześć L. · Colchester · Leiden · Utrecht · Münster · POLAND · London · Rotterdam · THE NETHERLANDS · Bocholt · Wesel · Magdeburg · Wittenberg · Antwerp · Cologne · Mansfeld · Liegnitz · SILESIA · Raków · Ghent · Maastricht · HESSE · Allstedt · Frankenhausen · Jauer · Pínczów · Cassel · Brussels · Liege · Aachen · Marburg · Mühlhausen · Orlamünde · Rogow · Cambray · Erfurt · Zwickau · Cracow · Lwów · Rouen · Frankfurt · Prague · GALICIA · Mainz · Würzburg · BOHEMIA · Olomouc · MORAVIA · Worms · Heidelberg · Nürnberg · Tabor · Austerlitz · FRANCE · Speyer · Nicolsburg · Auspitz · Paris · Metz · Ingolstadt · Regensburg · Hagenau · Esslingen · Passau · Vienna · Strassburg · Rottenburg · Ulm · Augsburg · Freistadt · HUNGARY · Orléans · Memmingen · Steyr · AUSTRIA · TRANSYLVANIA · Salzburg · IMPERIAL · Debreczen · Schaffhausen · Schleitheim · BAVARIA · Nagyvárad · Basel · Waldshut · Rattenberg · Kolozsvár · Zolfingen · Zürich · Constance · Schwatz · Veszprém · Torda · Maros-Vásárhely · Zollikon · St. Gall · Innsbruck · Gyulafehervar · Bern · Chur · Appenzell · Klausen · Nagyszeben · SWISS CONFEDERATION · Ilanz · Davos · TYROL · Kronstadt · GRISONS · Geneva · Locarno · Chiavenna · Trent · Pécs · Lyons · SAVOY · Vicenza · Treviso · OTTOMAN · Vienne · Milan · Asola · Padua · Venice · Grenoble · PIEDMONT · EMPIRE · Nérac · Alessandria · Modena · Ferrara · Toulouse · Bologna · Florence · Siena · Ragusa · Rome

Legend:
Anabaptist Concentrations & Movement
Antitrinitarian, Socinian Concentrations & Movement
+−+−+− Boundary of the Empire

51

PLATE 26

THE REFORMATION IN THE BRITISH ISLES

Henry VIII
By Hans Holbein the Younger

A number of factors contributed to the Reformation in England. The work of John Wyclif (d. 1384) and the movement he founded, the Lollards, must be noted. Wyclif, associated with the University of Oxford through most of his life, aimed at reformation of the English Church during the period of the Avignon papacy. His followers, called Lollards and given to vernacular preaching and Scripture reading, concentrated in the eastern counties and continued as an underground movement right up to the sixteenth century. These same eastern counties provided the bulk of the students at the University of Cambridge which was a seed plot for Reformation thinking in the sixteenth century.

Christian Humanism provided another spur to reform in England, as in northern Europe. The great universities of Oxford and Cambridge were centers, and from them, especially Cambridge, the future reformers came. One must also note the forces of national sentiment and anticlericalism used by Henry VIII. The appearance of Tyndale's English New Testament in 1525 aided in the cause of reform.

The personal aims of Henry VIII must also be considered. His concern for a male heir plus his growing distaste for his wife, Catherine of Aragon, led to protracted annulment or divorce proceedings, and eventually to a split with Rome and the establishment of a national church. Henry himself remained doctrinally orthodox, except on papal supremacy.

The plate indicates the county divisions of Henry as well as the reorganized ecclesiastical structure. We also note representative greater monasteries which Henry closed, thus removing potential trouble spots while at the same time acquiring vast tracts of land for the crown. His policies were opposed in several areas. The Pilgrimage of Grace, for example, of 1536 roused much of the northern part of the country, but was crushed by early 1537.

On Henry's death (1547) Edward ruled briefly, and Protestantism flourished, becoming deeply enough rooted so that the Catholic reaction led by Mary (1553-58) could not destroy it. Under Elizabeth I (1558-1603) an attempt was made to find the *via media* that has marked Anglicanism since that time.

In Scotland the work of John Knox is of greatest significance. The centers of St. Andrews, site of Wishart's martyrdom and Knox's preaching, Perth, another preaching spot of Knox, and the University of Glasgow are of special importance.

PLATE 27

THE REFORMATION IN FRANCE

The paths of Reformation had been prepared in France, as in other lands by the work of Christian Humanists. Jacques LeFevre d'Etaples (d. 1536) is the most notable example.

The greatest figure who moved beyond Humanism to Reformation was John Calvin. Born in Noyon, educated in Paris, Orléans, and Bourges, Calvin fled from persecution in Paris in 1533 and found refuge for the moment in Angoulême. After the publication of his *Institutes of the Christian Religion* in 1536 he visited Ferrara briefly and then, en route to Strassburg, was prevailed upon by Farel to stay in Geneva. Expelled two years later he assisted Bucer in Strassburg. The years in this Alsatian city were among his happiest. He ministered to the French Protestant refugees and taught theology. He also learned how a city could be reformed and added some theological themes to his stock. They would appear in later editions of the *Institutes*. Returning to Geneva in 1541, Calvin extended his influence back to his native land through the *Institutes,* and through the students and refugees who often came to the Swiss city from France.

By 1555 there was a Reformed congregation in Paris and by 1559 there were over seventy such congregations in France and a General Synod met and adopted a strongly Calvinistic confession of faith. The French Protestants had, since the late 1550's, been called Huguenots.

A combination of religious, national, political, and economic factors tore France in pieces as no less than eight wars were fought, all concerned in one way or another with Huguenot freedom. There was a lull in 1570 when the Peace of St. Germaine was signed. It allowed the nobility freedom of worship and gave the Huguenot commoners two places of worship in each governmental district of France. Four cities, Cognac, La Charité, Montaban, and La Rochelle (underlined on the plate), were given over to Huguenot control.

War broke out again however, as thousands of Protestants were killed in the St. Bartholomew's Day massacre in August 1572. In 1598 the Edict of Nantes officially ended the struggle and gave Huguenots the right of public office and public worship except in Paris, Rheims, Toulouse, Lyons, and Dijon. Certain cities were set aside as places of refuge. The most important are noted on the plate.

The Huguenots prospered until the Edict of Nantes was revoked in 1685 by Louis XIV. Thousands of their number left France to settle in Holland, Prussia, England, and America.

PLATE 28

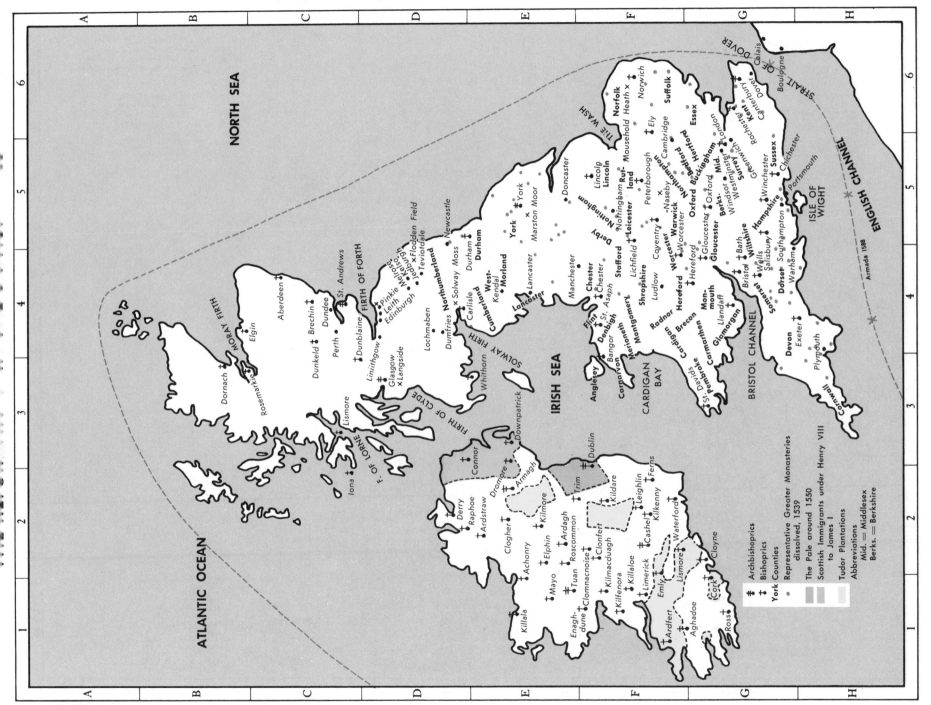

NORTH SEA

ATLANTIC OCEAN

IRISH SEA

ENGLISH CHANNEL

BRISTOL CHANNEL

CARDIGAN BAY

MORAY FIRTH

FIRTH OF FORTH

FIRTH OF CLYDE

F. OF LORNE

SOLWAY FIRTH

THE WASH

STRAIT OF DOVER

Armada 1588

Scotland

Dornach ✝
Rosemarkie •
Elgin •
Aberdeen •
Dunkeld ✝ Brechin ✝
Perth • Dundee •
St. Andrews ✝
Iona ✝
Lismore ✝
Glasgow • ✕ Langside
Dunblaine ✝
Linlithgow ✝
Leith • Edinburgh ✝
Pinkie •
Melrose ✕
Jedburgh ✕
Floddent Field ✕
Teviotdale
Lochmaben •
Dumfries • ✕ Solway Moss
Whithorn ✝
Carlisle ✝

Northumberland
Newcastle •
Durham ✝ **Durham**
Doncaster •
York ✝ ✕ Marston Moor
Lancaster •
Manchester •
West-
Morland
Cumberland
Kendal •
Lancaster

Chester ✝ **Chester**
St. Asaph ✝
Denbigh • **Denbigh**
Flint • **Flint**
Bangor ✝ **Merioneth**
Carnarvon • **Carnarvon**
Anglesey
Montgomery
Radnor
Cardigan • **Cardigan**
Brecon • **Brecon**
St. Davids ✝ **Pembroke**
Carmarthen • **Carmarthen**
Glamorgan
Llandaff ✝
Mon-mouth

Lincoln ✝ **Lincoln**
Nottingham • **Nottingham**
Rut-land
Peterborough ✝
✕ Naseby
Northampton
Leicester • **Leicester**
Derby
Lichfield ✝
Coventry •
Worcester ✝ **Worcester**
Warwick Warwick •
Shropshire
Ludlow •
Hereford ✝ **Hereford**
Gloucester ✝ **Gloucester**

Ely ✝
Cambridge ✝ **Cambridge**
Oxford ✕ Oxford ✝
Oxford **Buckingham**
Bedford
Hertford
Mid.
Windsor • Westminster ✝
London •
Berks.

Norfolk
Mousehold Heath ✕
Norwich ✝
Suffolk
Essex
Greenwich •
Rochester ✝
Canterbury ✝ Dover •
Kent
Calais •
Boulogne •

Somerset
Bath ✝
Wells ✝
Salisbury ✝
Wiltshire
Warham ✕
Dorset
Winchester ✝
Hampshire
Southampton •
Portsmouth •
ISLE OF WIGHT
Chichester ✝
Sussex
Guildford •
Bristol ✝

Devon
Exeter ✝
Plymouth •
Cornwall

Ireland
Derry ✝
Raphoe ✝
Clogher ✝
Connor ✝
Down patrick ✝
Dromore ✝
Armagh ✝
Kilmore ✝
Ardagh ✝
Trim
Ardstraw ✝
Achonry ✝
Elphin ✝
Roscommon •
Kildare ✝
Dublin ✝
Mayo ✝
Tuan ✝
Clonfert ✝
Clonmacnoise ✝
Killala ✝
Enagh-dune ✝
Kilmacduagh ✝
Kilfenora ✝
Killaloe ✝
Limerick ✝
Ardfert ✝
Ratass ✝
Emly ✝
Cashel ✝
Leighlin ✝
Ferns ✝
Kilkenny ✝
Lismore ✝
Waterford ✝
Cloyne ✝
Cork ✝
Aghadoe ✝
Ross ✝

Legend
✝ Archbishoprics
✝ Bishoprics
✝ York Counties
• Representative Greater Monasteries dissolved, 1539
The Pale around 1550
Scottish Immigrants under Henry VIII to James I
Tudor Plantations
Abbreviations
Mid. = Middlesex
Berks. = Berkshire

53

PLATE 27

THE REFORMATION IN FRANCE

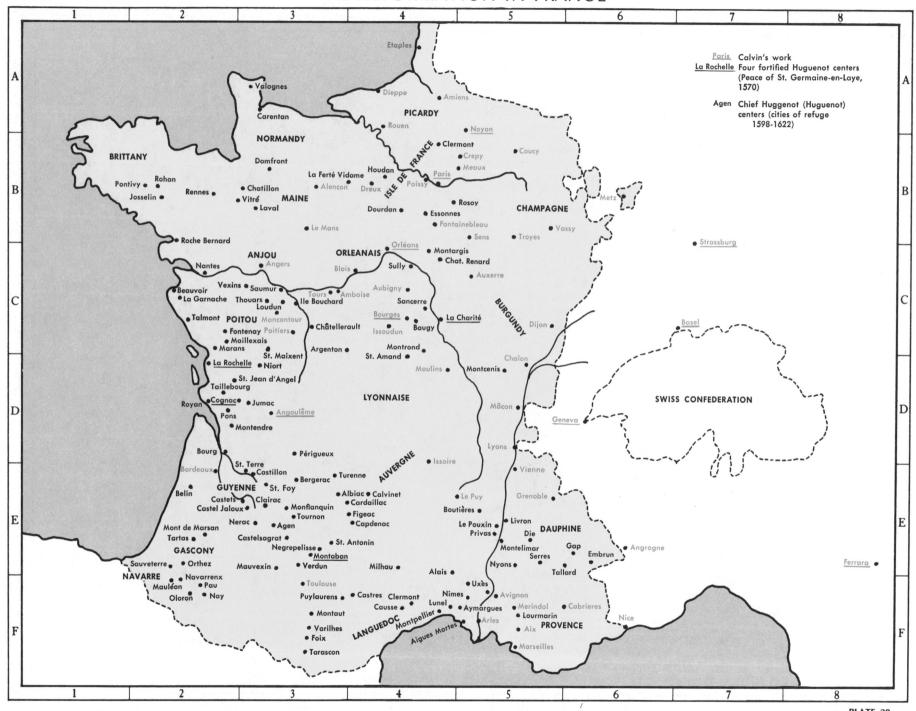

Paris — Calvin's work
La Rochelle — Four fortified Huguenot centers (Peace of St. Germaine-en-Laye, 1570)

Agen — Chief Huggenot (Huguenot) centers (cities of refuge 1598-1622)

Etaples
Valognes
Dieppe
Amiens
Carentan
PICARDY
NORMANDY
Rouen
Noyon
Clermont
Coucy
Domfront
Crepy
La Ferté Vidame
Houdan
Meaux
Alençon
Dreux
Poissy
Paris
BRITTANY
Rohan
Chatillon
MAINE
Pontivy
Rennes
Vitré
Laval
Rosoy
CHAMPAGNE
Josselin
Dourdan
Essonnes
Metz
Le Mans
Fontainebleau
Vassy
Roche Bernard
Sens
Troyes
Strassburg
Nantes
ANJOU
Angers
ORLEANAIS
Orléans
Montargis
Blois
Sully
Chat. Renard
Vexins
Saumur
Aubigny
Auxerre
Beauvoir
Thouars
Tours
Amboise
Sancerre
BURGUNDY
La Garnache
Loudun
Ile Bouchard
Basel
Talmont
POITOU
Moncontour
Châtellerault
Bourges
La Charité
Dijon
Fontenay
Poitiers
Baugy
Maillexais
Issoudun
Montrond
SWISS CONFEDERATION
Marans
Argenton
St. Amand
Chalon
St. Maixent
La Rochelle
Niort
LYONNAISE
Moulins
Montcenis
St. Jean d'Angel
Taillebourg
Royan
Cognac
Jumac
Angoulême
Mâcon
Pons
Geneva
Montendre
Bourg
Périgueux
Lyons
Bordeaux
St. Terre
Issoire
AUVERGNE
Castillon
Bergerac
Turenne
Vienne
Belin
GUYENNE
St. Foy
Grenoble
Castets
Clairac
Albiac
Calvinet
Le Puy
Castel Jaloux
Monflanquin
Cardaillac
Boutières
Nerac
Tournon
Figeac
Livron
DAUPHINE
Mont de Marsan
Agen
Capdenac
Le Pouxin
Die
Tartas
Castelsagrat
Privas
GASCONY
Negrepelisse
St. Antonin
Montelimar
Gap
Embrun
Sauveterre
Orthez
Montaban
Verdun
Milhau
Serres
Angrogne
NAVARRE
Mauvexin
Alais
Nyons
Tallard
Mauléon
Navarrenx
Pau
Uxès
Ferrara
Oloron
Nay
Toulouse
Nimes
Avignon
Merindol
Cabrieres
Puylaurens
Castres
Clermont
Lunel
Aymargues
Lourmarin
Nice
Causse
Arles
Montaut
LANGUEDOC
Montpellier
PROVENCE
Varilhes
Aix
Foix
Aigues Mortes
Marseilles
Tarascon

54

PLATE 28

THE REFORMATION IN THE NETHERLANDS

This was Spanish territory at the beginning of the period, but the oppressive taxes levied by Philip II, his attempts to centralize the government at the expense of local freedom, and religious oppression (the Inquisition was introduced in 1559) all contributed to a major and lengthy revolt.

The war lasted from 1567, when the Duke of Alva arrived with 10,000 Spanish troops, to 1609. During this protracted combat the Spanish proved themselves able to defeat the Dutch in open land combat while the Dutch were not to be excelled in the defense of walled cities or in sea warfare. Their cities in the north were defended by walls and also by marshes and canals. Their domination of the sea forced the invaders to use overland supply routes and enabled the Dutch eventually to control the coasts. A whole series of Spanish commanders attempted by force and diplomacy to control the Low Countries. They failed due to the topography of the north, the tenacious character of the Dutch, and also to the interference of their king, Philip II of Spain. This ruler persisted in meddling in affairs which he quite plainly did not understand. Philip was also distracted by his problems with Elizabeth of England (the Armada sailed to destruction in 1588), with Henry of Navarre in France, with the Turks and the Morisco rebellion in Spain itself, and finally with the problems of his colonies in the New World.

The northern provinces were mainly Protestant, the southern, Catholic, but they were united in 1576 and 1577 by the Spanish atrocities at Antwerp. This Union of Brussels was dissolved by Spanish diplomacy in 1579 into the Union of Arras (Catholic) and the Union of Utrecht (Protestant). In 1581 the northern provinces declared themselves independent from Spain and made William of Orange their leader. William's son, Maurice of Nassau, succeeded him and led the north to virtual independence by 1609. This territory came to dominate the commerce and industry of this part of Europe and remained strongly Protestant. The South, heavily damaged by the long war, dropped behind in the commercial competition. Although Protestantism had found its earliest adherents there, the Catholic revival vigorously suppressed them and the territory became a stronghold of the Counter-Reformation. The split of the Low Countries by the Twelve Years' Truce of 1609 has lasted to this day: Holland in the North is still Protestant; Belgium remains Roman Catholic.

PLATE 29

THE COUNTER-REFORMATION (to 1648)

In this era the Roman Catholics moved to reform the church from within and also to recapture the territories lost to Protestantism. A pattern for inner reform was close at hand in Spanish Catholicism. Purified and hardened by generations of conflict with the Mohammedans, the Spanish Church had revived the best of medieval Catholic mystical piety (e.g. St. Teresa and St. John of the Cross), and also refurbished the intellectual system of Scholasticism. These patterns were brought north over the Pyrenees.

The papacy itself changed markedly during this period. It was with Paul III (1534-1549) that the Counter-Reformation really began. Though he was also a Renaissance type figure still he did appoint a commission to study reform in which the conservative position eventually carried the day. He also confirmed the Jesuit Order in 1540, and in 1542 reluctantly approved the use of the Inquisition in Italy and called the Council of Trent. With Paul IV (1555-59) there was a definite turning point in Roman Catholicism. He was an ardent, serious, and strongly anti-Protestant leader who reformed the papacy and the city of Rome.

The three major weapons or arms in the attempt to recover the lost ground and purify the church were the Jesuit Order, the Inquisition, and the Council of Trent.

The recognition of the Jesuits in 1540 by Paul III was of major significance in the reformation of Catholicism and the attack upon Protestantism. These disciplined men were the shock troops of the Counter-Reformation. One of the means used effectively to reclaim and reform was education. Protestantism was virtually surrounded by Jesuit schools. It was through education that the battle was won in some areas.

In lands where there was sufficient popular support, the Inquisition, a tool already widely utilized in Spain, was reintroduced. In Italy, for example, the Reformation was swept away in ten bloody years (1542-52) by this arm of the church.

The Council of Trent (1543-63) represents another method of dealing with the religious problems of the sixteenth century. A strongly conservative, anti-Protestant stance was taken at this lengthy meeting.

The Counter-Reformation also was furthered by military means, some successful, others not. A prime example of a combination of national and religious warfare is the Spanish Armada (1588).

PLATE 30

William of Orange
From a painting by Mierevelt

Pope Paul III
From an old woodcut, Gotha Museum

THE REFORMATION IN THE NETHERLANDS

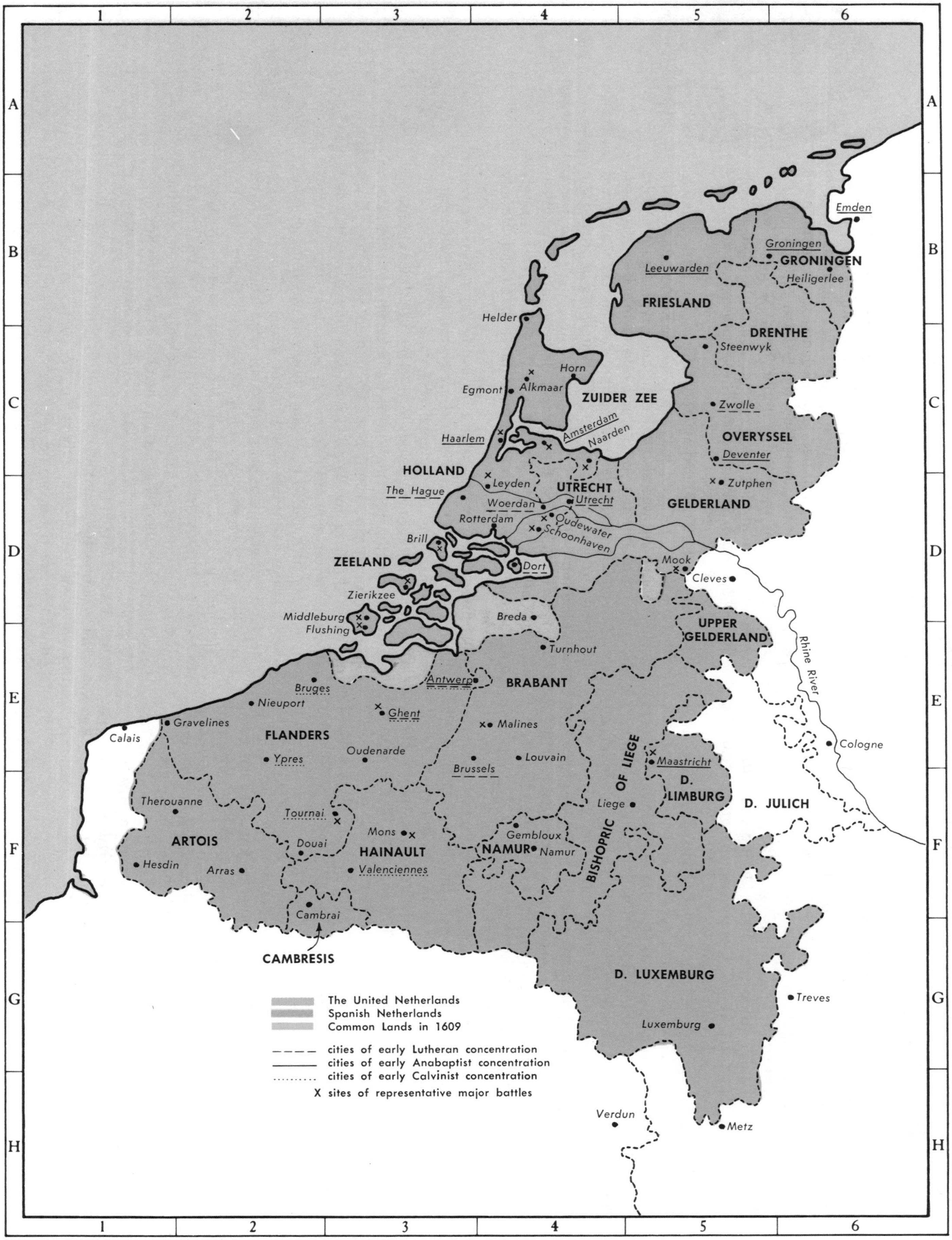

Emden

Groningen · GRONINGEN
Heiligerlee

DRENTHE
Steenwyk

OVERYSSEL
Zwolle · Deventer × Zutphen

GELDERLAND

FRIESLAND
Leeuwarden

Cleves

Rhine River

Cologne

Treves

D. JULICH

UPPER
GELDERLAND

Mook ×

Maastricht
D. LIMBURG

Metz

D. LUXEMBURG

Luxemburg

ZUIDER ZEE

Horn
Alkmaar ×
Egmont ×
Amsterdam × Naarden

UTRECHT
Utrecht
Oudewater ×
Woerden × Schoonhaven ×
Leyden ×

Helder

BISHOPRIC OF LIEGE

Liege
Namur
NAMUR · Namur
Gembloux

Turnhout

Breda

BRABANT

Louvain

Verdun

Haarlem

HOLLAND
The Hague
Rotterdam · Dort

Brill

Antwerp

Malines ×

Brussels

Oudenarde

Mons ×
HAINAULT
Valenciennes ×

Middleburg ×××
Flushing
Zierikzee

ZEELAND

Ghent ×

FLANDERS
Ypres ×
Nieuport
Bruges

Tournai ×

Douai

Cambrai

CAMBRESIS

Gravelines

Calais

Therouanne

ARTOIS
Hesdin · Arras

The United Netherlands
Spanish Netherlands
Common Lands in 1609

- - - cities of early Lutheran concentration
——— cities of early Anabaptist concentration
········ cities of early Calvinist concentration
× sites of representative major battles

PLATE 29

THE COUNTER-REFORMATION (to 1648)

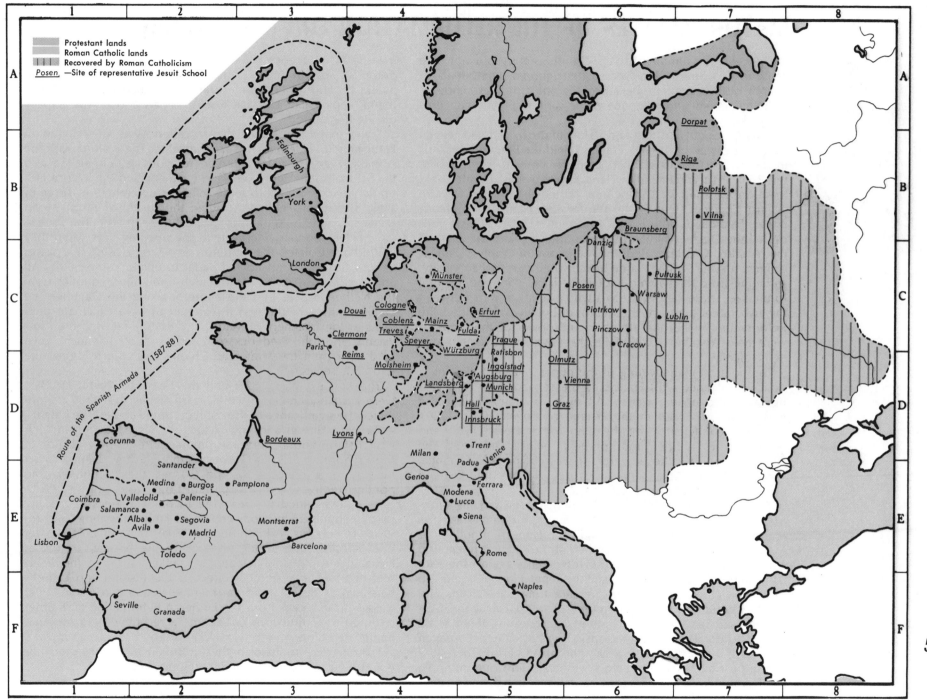

Protestant lands
Roman Catholic lands
Recovered by Roman Catholicism
Posen —Site of representative Jesuit School

Route of the Spanish Armada (1587-88)

Edinburgh
York
London

Dorpat
Riga
Polotsk
Vilna
Braunsberg
Danzig
Pultusk
Posen
Warsaw
Piotrkow
Lublin
Pinczow
Cracow
Olmutz
Vienna
Graz

Münster
Douai
Cologne
Coblenz
Mainz
Erfurt
Clermont
Treves
Fulda
Paris
Speyer
Würzburg
Prague
Reims
Molsheim
Ratisbon
Ingolstadt
Landsberg
Augsburg
Munich
Hall
Innsbruck
Lyons

Trent
Milan
Padua
Venice
Bordeaux
Genoa
Ferrara
Corunna
Modena
Santander
Lucca
Medina
Burgos
Pamplona
Siena
Coimbra
Valladolid
Palencia
Salamanca
Segovia
Alba
Avila
Montserrat
Madrid
Lisbon
Toledo
Barcelona
Rome
Naples
Seville
Granada

57

PLATE 30

MAJOR BATTLES OF THE REFORMATION ERA (16th century)

The Warrior Colleoni
From a statue by
Verrocchio

The religious tumult of the sixteenth century did not take place in a vacuum. One factor often ignored by students of church history, perhaps because it is not "spiritual" enough, is the movement and influence of the various military concerns of the day.

The houses of Hapsburg and Valois mutually claimed several areas (see plates 19 and 31). Francis I held the Burgundian lands in the north; Charles claimed them by descent from Charles the Bold. Francis demanded Flanders and Artois; Charles held them. In the southwest Francis supported the King of Navarre against Charles's right to the territory annexed by his grandfather, Ferdinand. Both hoped to dominate Italy. Francis controlled the Duchy of Milan; Charles argued that it was part of the empire. Charles ruled the Kingdom of Naples; Francis claimed it as heir of the Anjou house. Their personal animosity, springing from their contest for imperial election, added fuel to the fire. These factors led to a whole series of wars between the two rulers that disturbed Europe, but that also aided the Reformation in that the attention and power of the emperor were held to other areas while the German movement was in its infancy.

The political maneuvering of the popes, usually following a policy of alliance with Francis as the second most powerful figure, is also of importance. An example of this balance of power policy is seen in the League of Cognac (May 1526). Having been defeated by the emperor at Pavia (1525) and released after a brief imprisonment, Francis organized the League to oppose the emperor. It was composed of France, Venice, Florence, Milan, *and* the papacy. Henry VIII of England favored it but did not join officially.

The incursions of Suleiman the Magnificent and his Ottoman hordes were another important factor, for much the same reason. After defeating the cream of the Hungarian nobility at Mohacs in 1526 the road to central Europe seemed open. The continent was now aroused and made defense against the Turk its common cause and managed to repel him at Vienna in 1529. The almost unrelenting pressure from the Balkans and the Mediterranean forced the emperor to appeal to the German Protestants for support rather than crushing them as he wished to do. The Turkish expansion was actually encouraged by Francis I, who saw in it a way to harm Charles. There is a strong possibility that the French embassies in Constantinople in 1525 and 1528 encouraged the Balkan campaigns of Suleiman. Later the French called upon the Turks to attack the emperor by sea. In 1535 Francis actually made a treaty with Suleiman, and in 1543 the Turkish fleet, under *Francis'* command, took Nice. He was also in alliance with the papacy during this period

Some major battles of the so-called Wars of Religion in France and the Netherlands are indicated. These along with the Armada were efforts at a forced religious settlement. So also the Schmalcaldic War (1546-7) in Germany and the War of Liberation mark attempts to settle religious differences by force of arms. The Schmalcaldic War pitted the Elector of Saxony, John Frederick, and Philip of Hesse against the emperor. The Protestants failed to move decisively in the opening days when they could have isolated the emperor simply by closing the passes to Italy. Instead they allowed papal troops to come north and an imperial army of 10,000 to march three hundred miles from the Netherlands to join the emperor along the Danube. The Danube phase of the war threatened to be a stalemate until news of the treachery of Maurice of Saxony reached the Protestants, and John Frederick marched north to defend his own lands. This split the army, and Charles was able to defeat the two parts separately.

The Knights' War (1522) and the Peasants' Revolt (1524-5) were certainly crucial for their participants, but they do not match the significance of the conflicts noted above. The knights, under von Hutten and von Sickingen, wished to regain their feudal status and at the same time acquire the rich estates of the Archbishop of Trier (Treves). Although they claimed to act because of a concern for the Gospel, their economic and political motives were transparent. Both Protestant and Catholic princes joined to crush the revolt. The peasants, taking false encouragement from certain of Luther's writings and refusing to note his "Admonition to Peace," rose in 1524-5. After brief success, due to the absence of the princes' troops at Pavia, they were badly defeated at Frankenhausen by the newly returned mercenaries. One effect of this disaster and Luther's harsh words against them was that the greater part of the lower classes turned away from the Lutheran Reformation and either returned to Catholicism or became a receptive field for Anabaptist teachings.

For reference to major battles in Britain and the Netherlands one should note plates 28 and 29 respectively.

PLATE 31

58

MAJOR BATTLES OF THE REFORMATION ERA (16th century)

Boundary of the Empire ┼┼┼
France
Hapsburg holdings
Areas claimed by Chas. V and Francis I
Ottoman Empire
Underlining:
Turkish battle site
Hapsburg-Valois battle
Wars of Religion: French, Dutch
Schmalcaldic War and War of Liberation
Peasants' and Knights' Wars, 1524,5, and 1522

SCOTLAND
Donegal Bay
Firth of Forth
IRELAND
ENGLAND
FLANDERS
ARTOIS
See detail map on Netherlands

Bremen
Drakenburg
Sievershausen
Magdeburg
Flushing
Brill
Gravelines
Bruges
Calais
Antwerp
Ghent
Tournai
Cateau-Cambresis
Bologne
Havre
Montreuil
Hesdin
Cambray
St. Quentin
Trier
Soissons
Frankenhausen
Muhlberg
Ebernburg
St. Denis
Paris
Verdun
Landstuhl
Dreux
Metz
Strassburg
St. Dizier
Toul
Waldshut
Ratisbon
Ingolstadt
THE EMPIRE

Route of the Spanish Armada (1587-88)
Montcontour
La Rochelle
BURGUNDY
Vienna
TRANSYLVANIA
MOLDAVIA
Corunna
Jarnac
FRANCE
Guns
Gran
Buda
Santander
Fuenterrabia
NAVARRE
Valence
Novara
Turin
Milan
Bicocca
Agnadello
Stuhlweissenburg
WALLACHIA
Avignon
Ceresole
Marignano
Pavia
Funfkirchen
Mohacs
Lisbon
PORTUGAL
SPAIN
Perpignan
Marseilles
Nice
Landriano
Genoa
Parma
Florence
Semlin
Belgrade
REPUBLIC OF VENICE
OTTOMAN
Cadiz
CORSICA
Rome
PAPAL STATES
Constantinople
EMPIRE
Aversa
Napies
NAPLES
SARDINIA
Lepanto
Oran
Algiers
Bizerta
SICILY
Nauplia
Bona
Goletta
Tunis
Monemvasia
Rhodes
Famagusta

59

PLATE 31

THE THIRTY YEARS' WAR AND THE PEACE OF WESTPHALIA (1648)

Gustavus Adolphus
By Jacob of Delff

The Peace of Augsburg (1555) did not end the conflict in central Europe; it only provided a breathing space. Hostilities bubbling beneath the surface broke out in 1618.

The Thirty Years' War, generally divided into Bohemian, Danish, Swedish, and Swedish-French periods, depending upon either the place of major conflict or the leading powers involved, was a disaster for the mid-continent. Rival armies marched back and forth, fighting occasionally, plundering continually. Great military leaders appeared, to shine for a moment, only to fall again. The paths and areas of battle of some of them are shown on the plate (e.g. Gustavus Adolphus, Wallenstein, and Ernst of Mansfeld).

The territorial expansion of Protestantism had reached its widest range in central Europe around 1566, and then had begun to recede before the onrush of an aggressive Counter-Reformation. Innumerable incidents fanned the sparks of hostility. The repression of evangelical worship in Donauwörth in 1606 after the Protestants had stoned a Catholic procession typifies the rising tension. A Protestant "Union" of 1608 was countered by a Catholic "League" in 1609. The actual military conflict began in Bohemia where after a period of initial success the Protestants were defeated near Prague by a Catholic army led by Baron Tilly. The Palatinate was invaded and reclaimed by force of arms for Catholicism.

The Protestants fared no better in the north where Ernst of Mansfeld was defeated at Dessau by Wallenstein. Mansfeld retreated to the southeast, hoping to join Bethlen Gabor. The other Protestant of significance in this phase, King Christian IV of Denmark, was defeated by Tilly at Lutter in 1626.

The Catholics attempted to recover ecclesiastical property lost since 1552 by the Edict of Restitution (1629) and would have succeeded but for internal dissension. Politics and military considerations make for strange alliances. We have already seen how a pope, Clement VII, could be allied with Francis I against the emperor at the very moment when Francis was also allied with Suleiman. During the Thirty Years' War we have the odd sight of a Catholic Cardinal, Richelieu of France, siding with the Protestants of the Grisons area and warning the Pope that he would go to war if the Valtellina Valley was not cleared of Spanish and papal troops. This valley was of crucial importance as a gateway through the Alps for troop movement. Richelieu was engaged in fighting the Huguenots until 1628, but he was also desperately concerned with the claims of the Hapsburgs and fought the Austrians and Spanish at every opportunity. This conflict dragged on to 1631 and illustrates admirably the complexity of the whole struggle.

In the meantime the Swedish ruler, Gustavus Adolphus (d. 1632), impelled by hopes of making the Baltic a Swedish sea, and of aiding his fellow Lutherans, landed on the north German coast. Moved by the fall of Magdeburg to Tilly (1631) the north German Protestants finally united, and with Gustavus they defeated Tilly at Breitenfeld (1631). The plate indicates Gustavus' triumphant march to the Rhine. Wallenstein and Gustavus met at Lützen (Nov. 1632). The imperial forces were defeated although Gustavus himself was killed.

The war ground on. It became apparent after the Battle of Nördlingen (1634) that the Catholics could not hold northern Germany, nor the Protestants, southern. This ought to have ended the war, but it rumbled on for thirteen terrible years, until, after lengthy negotiations, a spirit of compromise prevailed and finally, in October of 1648, the Peace of Westphalia was signed.

According to this document certain powers acquired additional land. For example, France received Metz, Verdun, Toul, and the crown lands in Alsace; Sweden gained a beachhead in Pomerania; Brandenburg acquired eastern Pomerania and several bishoprics. The document also recognized the independence of Switzerland and the United Provinces in the Low Countries. No gains, however, could pay for the losses caused by the protracted conflict.

Although it had ostensibly been a war of religion, the bloodletting did not appreciably alter the ecclesiastical picture of the continent. The Peace of Westphalia reaffirmed the Peace of Augsburg and added the Reformed Churches to its recognized list. The date for fixing religious ownership was set at January 1624. With the exception of the lands of the Austrian Hapsburgs where the Counter-Reformation gains were to be allowed to stand, the areas that were Protestant or Catholic in 1624 were to remain so. The division thus established has not been radically altered to this day. (For the general religious division see plate 24.)

60

PLATE 32

THE THIRTY YEARS' WAR AND THE PEACE OF WESTPHALIA (1648)

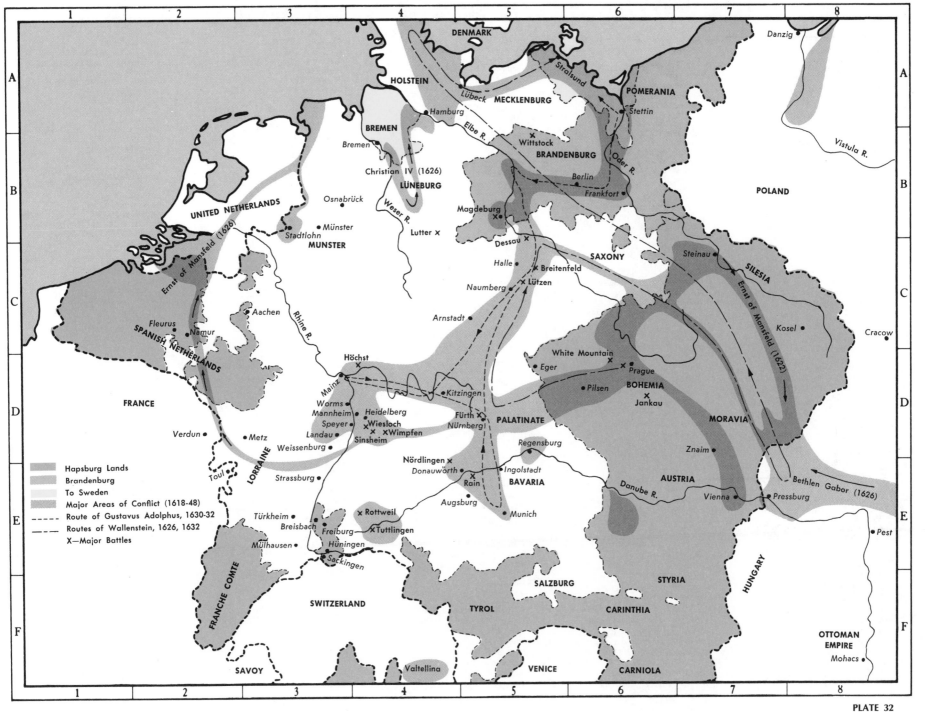

DENMARK

HOLSTEIN

Stralsund

Lübeck
MECKLENBURG
POMERANIA

BREMEN
Hamburg
Stettin

Bremen
Elbe R.
Wittstock
BRANDENBURG
Oder R.

Christian IV (1626)
LÜNEBURG
Berlin
Frankfort

Osnabrück
Vistula R.

UNITED NETHERLANDS
Weser R.
Magdeburg ×
POLAND

Stadtlohn
Münster
Lutter ×
SAXONY
Steinau

MUNSTER
Dessau ×
SILESIA

Ernst of Mansfeld (1626)
Halle
Breitenfeld
Kosel

Aachen
Naumberg × Lützen
Cracow

Fleurus
Arnstadt
Ernst of Mansfeld (1622)

SPANISH
Rhine R.
White Mountain

Namur
NETHERLANDS
Höchst ×
Eger • Prague ×
BOHEMIA

FRANCE
Mainz
Kitzingen
Pilsen
Jankau ×
MORAVIA

Worms
Heidelberg
Fürth ×
PALATINATE
Znaim

Verdun
Metz
Mannheim • Speyer Wiesloch × Nürnberg
Bethlen Gabor (1626)

Landau × Wimpfen
Regensburg

Weissenburg Sinsheim
Nördlingen ×
Ingolstadt
AUSTRIA

LORRAINE
Strassburg
Donauwörth ×
Rain ×
BAVARIA
Danube R.
Vienna
Pressburg

Toul
Türkheim
Augsburg
Munich
Pest

Verdun
Breisbach
Rottweil ×
Freiburg
Tuttlingen ×
SALZBURG
STYRIA
HUNGARY

Mülhausen
Hüningen
CARINTHIA

Säckingen
SWITZERLAND
TYROL
CARNIOLA
OTTOMAN
EMPIRE

FRANCHE COMTE
Mohacs

SAVOY
Valtellina
VENICE

Legend:
- Hapsburg Lands
- Brandenburg
- To Sweden
- Major Areas of Conflict (1618-48)
- - - - Route of Gustavus Adolphus, 1630-32
- — · — Routes of Wallenstein, 1626, 1632
- X—Major Battles

PLATE INDEX

TEXT INDEX